MILITARY TO FEDERAL CAREER GUIDE, 2ND EDITION

FEDERAL RESUME WRITING FOR VETERANS

KATHRYN TROUTMAN

Published by The Resume Place, Inc.
Baltimore, MD
Phone: (888) 480-8265
Email: resume@resume-place.com
Website: www.resume-place.com

Published by The Resume Place, Inc.
Baltimore, MD
Phone: (888) 480-8265
Email: resume@resume-place.com
Website: www.resume-place.com

Printed in the United States of America
Library of Congress Control Number: 2010928427

ISBN 13: 978-0-9824190-2-1
ISBN 10: 0-9824190-2-3

PUBLICATION TEAM:
Interior Design and Covers: Brian Moore
CD-ROM Designer: Brian Moore
Developmental Editors: Paulina Chen and Emily Troutman
Federal Resume Samples: Kathryn Troutman
CD-ROM Editor: Brian Moore
Indexer: L. Pilar Wyman

OTHER BOOKS BY KATHRYN TROUTMAN

Ten Steps to a Federal Job & CD-ROM, 2nd Ed.

Jobseeker's Guide, 4th Ed.

Federal Resume Guidebook & CD-ROM, 5th Ed.
(Published by Jist, Inc., Indianapolis, IN)

The Student's Federal Career Guide & CD-ROM
Co-authored with Emily K. Troutman

Creating Your High School Resume, 3rd Ed.
(Published by Jist, Inc., Indianapolis, IN)

ORDER BOOKS ONLINE @
WWW.RESUME-PLACE.COM

DEDICATION

For all the men and women of the U.S. Army, Navy, Air Force, Marine Corps, Coast Guard, and National Guard who dedicate their lives to our nation's defense.

Welcome home, Vets!

ACKNOWLEDGEMENTS

THANK YOU to the Veteran's Counselors, Military Transition Counselors, University Career Counselors, and other Career Professionals from around the world and with all of the services, who care about helping veterans apply for federal jobs and write their first federal resume. This book is designed to help YOU help THEM.

THANK YOU to every veteran that I advise or teach federal job search strategies. You have taught ME how important it is that this book be easy to read and understand, so that YOU can write the best federal resume and land a federal job.

THANK YOU TO JOHN BERRY, DIRECTOR OF OFFICE OF PERSONNEL MANAGEMENT AND BARRACK OBAMA, PRESIDENT OF THE UNITED STATES, for eliminating the narrative essay-style KSA questions and requesting that agencies use a <u>resume and cover letter</u> as the application for a federal job.

– Kathryn Troutman

TABLE OF CONTENTS

APPENDIX

CD-ROM CONTENT

CD-ROM TABLE OF CONTENTS
Federal Resume Samples in USAJOBS/ Outline Format in Word and PDF

- 26 Military to Federal Resume samples, including Outline Format federal resumes for USAJOBS and other resume builders.
- Other resume formats include: paper resume formats, corporate resumes, and job fair resume samples. Read the full list of samples on the following page.
- Glossary of Federal Employment Terms
- List of Federal Agency Names
- List of Federal Occupational Series and Job Titles
- Core Competencies for Marine Corps, Defense Logistics Agency, U.S. Dept. of Veterans Affairs, and Senior Executive Service
- White House Memoradum, 5/11/10, outlining the upcoming changes to the federal hiring system

RESUME SAMPLES ON CD-ROM

NAME	SERVICE	RANK	GRADE	TARGET OCCUPATIONAL SERIES AND TITLE		RESUME FORMAT
Billings	USCG	E-5	GS-05	1802	Transportation Security Officer	Outline Format
				0083	Police Officer	
				1810	Background Investigator	
				0086	Security Assistant	
Rodriguez	USMC	E-6	GS-07/09	301	Administration, Program Mgt.	Outline Format
				343	Management Analyst	
				501	Financial Administration	
				512	Internal Revenue Agent	
				560, 561 - Budget Analyst / Technician		
				2200	Admn work in Information Technology	
Tarka	USN	E-6	GS-09/11	343	Mgt. Analyst, Resource Mgt.	Outline Format
				346	Logistics Management	Air Force Builder
				2001	General Supply Specialist	Paper Federal
				2003, 2005 - Supply Mgt Analyst/Specialist		Corporate
				2010	Inventory Management Specialist	
Denton	USMC	E-5	GS-07	0343	Management and Program Analyst	Outline Format
Gannon	USAF	E-5	GS-05/07	0525	Accounting Technician	Outline Format
				1811	Special Agent	
Smith	USN	AT2	GS-05/07	FV-0856-F/G - Electronics Technician		Outline Format
				2210	Information Technology Specialist	
Logan	USANG	E-7/SFC	GS-09/11	0301	Administrative Officer	Outline Format
				0304	Management and Program Analyst	
Gilliam	USA	E-8	GS-12	0301	Administrative Officer	Outline Format
Benedetto	USA	CW-2	GS-09/11/12	2152	Air Traffic Controller	Outline Format
				2181	Airline Pilot / Helicopter Flight Instructor	USAjobs Resume
				2183	Aircraft Electronic Warfare Spec., Officer	
Perkins	USA	CW-4	GS-11/12/13	346	Logistics Management Specialist	Outline Format
				2181	Airline Pilot / Helicopter Flight Instructor	Navy Resume
				2183	Aircraft Electronic Warfare Spec., Officer	
MacArthur	USAR	CW-4	GS-11/12	201	Human Resources Specialist (Military)	Before Resume
						Outline Format
						Job Fair, 1 pg
						KSA
Roberts	USA	O-4	GS-13/14	301, 341 - Administration, Program Mgt. Spec.		Outline Format
				343	Management Analyst, Resource Mgt.	Corporate, 1 pg
				346	Logistics Management	Job Fair, 1 pg
				1102	Contracting, Procurement Specialist	
Lester	USANG	O-5	GS-13/14	301, 341 - Administration, Program Mgt.		Outline Format
				343	Management Analyst, Resource Mgt.	CPOL Resume
				346	Logistics Management	
				1101	Business, Industry Specialist	

Resume samples on CD-ROM to be updated regularly.

AUTHOR'S INTRODUCTION

As a former or current member of the U.S. armed forces, you have already demonstrated personal dedication, perseverance, and a strong commitment to service. Today the U.S. government is prepared to offer you new, economically competitive, and hopefully fulfilling employment opportunities. Your skills are currently in very high demand and can help the nation respond to complex global security threats.

There are several challenges to landing what are now recognized as the best jobs / careers in the country, and maybe even the world. First, you have to find the position that's right for you, and second, you have to write a federal resume that demonstrates you are at least minimally qualified for the job. YOU will have to make this happen.

Right now, your job is to read this book, study the resume samples, and write the best possible resume you can to match the job announcements you are interested in.

You, and only you, can take this first step.

On the other hand, you have several advantages working in your favor.

First, the government has numerous preference programs for both veterans and families of veterans. Because you are a veteran, your applications can receive a 5 or 10 points added to your application score. You can read about the veteran's preference points in the appendix of this book.

Secondly, President Obama has created a new initiative to provide jobs for returning veterans. On Nov. 9, 2009, President Obama signed an executive order launching a major veterans employment initiative to create an Interagency Council on Veterans Employment. The order establishes a Veterans Employment Program office within most federal agencies. These offices will be responsible for helping veterans identify employment opportunities within those federal agencies, providing feedback to veterans about their employment application status, and helping veterans recently employed by these agencies adjust to civilian life and a workplace culture often different from military service.

To view the Agency Directory Contact List for Veterans, go to:
http://www.fedshirevets.gov/AgencyDirectory/index.aspx

Finally, the application is getting easier. President Obama and Director John Berry of the Office of Personnel Management have written a White House Memo to all Department heads that they should request a resume (federal style – outline format) and cover letter as the application for a federal job. This is still very new, but the directive should improve the federal hiring process by eliminating the written essays / KSAs.

Finally, you now also have this book to give you an advantage in your job search. This book will help you write a federal resume that will hopefully get you at least the minimally-qualifying score of 70 on your federal application. The federal resume samples in this book and the methods to identify keywords and feature accomplishments will help you get minimally qualified, qualified, best qualified, referred to a federal job, selected for an interview, and HIRED into an excellent, stable federal career!

In an easy-to-follow, step-by-step process, this book will teach you:

- To write the federal resume in the Outline Format, so that it is easy to read

- That the TAP or private industry resume is NOT the same as a federal resume

- How to analyze vacancy announcements for qualifications and keywords

- How to understand federal job vacancy announcements

- To make a list of keywords to add into your resume

- To feature accomplishments in your resume, so you will stand out

- How to apply for federal jobs on USAJOBS and other online agencies

Military to Federal Career Guide is different from other resume books, because it presents a new, cutting-edge format for resume writing. You will learn how to write your Military to Federal Resume. **The Military to Federal Resume translates your military experience into federal job keywords and qualifications in a successful USAJOBS and federal resume builder application.**

Good luck with your job search,

Kathryn Troutman, *President*

The Resume Place, Inc.
www.resume-place.com

Veteran's website for federal jobs!
www.fedshirevets.gov

CHAPTER 1:

WRITE YOUR MILITARY TO FEDERAL RESUME

Getting started, finding your documents, writing your basic federal resume

THE WHITE HOUSE
Office of the Press Secretary
For Immediate Release May 11, 2010
May 11, 2010

MEMORANDUM FOR THE HEADS OF EXECUTIVE DEPARTMENTS AND AGENCIES

SUBJECT: Improving the Federal Recruitment and Hiring Process
To deliver the quality services and results the American people expect and deserve.

By the authority vested in me as President by the Constitution and the laws of the United States, including section 3301 of title 5, United States Code, I hereby direct the following:

Section 1. Directions to Agencies. Agency heads shall take the following actions no later than November 1, 2010:

(a) consistent with merit system principles and other requirements of title 5, United States Code, and subject to guidance to be issued by the Office of Personnel Management (OPM), adopt hiring procedures that:

1. eliminate any requirement that applicants respond to essay-style questions when submitting their initial application materials for any Federal job;

2. allow individuals to apply for Federal employment by submitting resumes and cover letters or completing simple, plain language applications, and assess applicants using valid, reliable tools.

Read the entire memorandum on the CD-ROM.

Note about the "resume and cover letter" recommendation in this memorandum:

The President is reminding the human resources specialists that Title 5, Merit Principles are still in place. Therefore, federal job seekers should use a federal resume, which is longer and more detailed than a private industry resume. The federal resume formats and techniques taught in this book will prove qualifications and ensure a fair, merit-based assessment of your skills and specialized experience.

WRITING YOUR FIRST BASIC
MILITARY TO FEDERAL RESUME

Your federal resume is the most important career document you will write as you pursue your new federal career after military service. According to federal human resources specialists, the Work Experience section in your resume is THE most important section of the resume, because it describes your experiences, knowledge, skills, and abilities. There are several challenges to landing what are now recognized as the best jobs / careers in the country, and maybe even the world. First, you have to find the position that's right for you, and second, you have to write a federal resume that demonstrates you are at least minimally qualified for the job. YOU will have to make this happen. Right now, your job is to read this book, study the resume samples, and write the best possible resume you can to match the job announcements you are interested in.

The federal resume will be your job application, your "examination" for the job, and sometimes even your interview.

The federal resume is NOT the same as the TAP or private industry resume.
Most civilian resumes are generic, with few specifics about actual military experience. The civilian resume is correct and preferred for private industry job searches as many corporate and small business managers do not understand military job duties, ranks, training, or situations.

The Military to Federal Resume can include some of your military experiences, if they are relevant for your federal job search. Your mission critical skills can help you to demonstrate that you are Qualified or even Best Qualified for a certain position.

For example, the Department of Homeland Security is now hiring thousands of border patrol employees. In such a case, your military history can give you a competitive edge. It is desirable to incorporate specific military details in your resume including rank, service name, base or post locations, operation names in which you served, relevant experiences with numbers and particulars, specialized training course titles, accomplishments, and quotes. Military job assignments will be written with a description of the military activities, operations, and duties.

MILITARY TO FEDERAL RESUME VS. TAP OR PRIVATE INDUSTRY RESUME:

MILITARY TO FEDERAL RESUME	TAP OR PRIVATE INDUSTRY RESUME
Names of bases, posts, and locations	No specifics about bases or posts, countries, or locations
Specific accomplishments	Accomplishments generalized
Description of technical work	General descriptions
Some military terminology okay	Military terminology decoded
Clearance listed	Clearance listed
Training described, including location of training, hours of training, title of course, certification (if any)	Training may or may not be included, depending on relevance to your new career objective.
Average length: 3 to 4 pages	Average length: 2 pages

RECOMMENDED FORMAT FOR FEDERAL RESUMES: OUTLINE FORMAT

All the case studies in the book are in Outline Format. The Outline Format is a highly successful, readable federal resume format effective in all of the resume builders. The Outline Format features small paragraphs, keywords, and accomplishments.

Key features of the Outline Format:

- Use ALL CAPS to highlight keywords and important skills for the job
- No formatting: no indentations or centering of text
- No bold, italics, bullets, underlines
- Flush left, ragged right (no justified copy)
- Small paragraphs (4-8 lines max)
- Use ALL CAPS to highlight headers
- Add accomplishments at the end of each job block
- Feature the last 10 years of Work History
- Easy to copy and paste into builders

Military Status:
U.S. Marine Corps
E-5, Helicopter Crew Chief, CH53

Qualifications:
Applying for positions based on One Year Specialized Experience AND
Bachelor's Degree in Government and Public Policy, *cum laude*.
- **Management and Program Analyst, GS-0343**
- **Target Grade level: GS-7**
- **Salary range:** 34,075.00 – 43,000 per year

Jeremy found the following FCIP opportunity that is located in the Office of Human Capital, GPO University, Washington, DC.

VACANCY ANNOUNCEMENT

Keywords from the Overview:
- Do you aspire to lead?
- Do you like to bring the best out of people?
- Do you focus on getting results?
- Do you like analyzing and solving problems?

Duties: (keywords are in bold)
During the program, participants will work in progressively complex work assignments.
The primary purpose of the work is to provide **line managers with objective information for making decisions** on the administrative and programmatic aspects of agency operations and management.
Participants apply analytical and evaluative methods and techniques to situations or issues concerning the **efficiency and effectiveness** of program operations and makes recommendations for improvement in work operations.
Participants will **develop new methods, organizational structures,** and **management processes.**
Participants will be required to **consult and advise program managers** on **methods and procedures,** management surveys, management reports, and control techniques.
Manage short or long term projects, lead teams for short term projects;
Develop life cycle cost analyses of projects or perform **cost benefit** or economic evaluations of current or projected programs.

Qualifications Required: (keywords in bold)
To minimally qualify for the PG-5 level, you must have one of the following:

A. 3 years of progressively responsible experience, 1 year of which was equivalent to at least GS-4, that demonstrate the ability to:

- **Analyze problems** to identify significant factors, gather pertinent data, and **recognize solutions;**
- **Plan and organize work;** and
- **Communicate effectively orally** and in writing.

JEREMY D. DENTON

1234 Anywhere Street
City, State, Zipcode
Phone: 555.555.5555
Email: jeremy.d.denton@gmail.com

NOTE: Keywords from the vacancy announcement are in ALL CAPS as headings in the Outline Format resume. Support the keyword headings in your description.

US Citizen
Social Security Number: XXX-XX-XXXX
Veterans Preference: 5 points, US Marine Corps, 08/2003 to 01/2008, honorable discharge
Security Clearance: Secret (active), Interim Top Secret (active)

OBJECTIVE: Job Announcement Number: 10-346057-rm
Job Title, Series & Grade: Program Analyst (Emerging Leader Program), PG-0343-05/09
Agency: Government Printing Office

PROFESSIONAL EXPERIENCE

08/2003-01/2008, U.S. MARINE CORPS.

08/2003-10/2004, U.S. MARINE CORPS BASIC TRAINING AND HELICOPTER TRAINING, various USMC US locations.

10/2004-01/2008, HELICOPTER CREW CHIEF; E-5, Sgt, 3rd Marine Air Wing, Marine Corps Air Station Miramar, San Diego, CA; Salary: $30,000; 40+ hours per week; Supervisor: Staff Sergeant Bernie Milton, (555) 555-5151, may contact.

TEAM LEAD / FLIGHT CREW MEMBER: Planned, organized, led, and performed maintenance on CH-53E Super Stallion helicopters, including during Operation Iraqi Freedom. Supported more than 2,000 sorties in several major campaigns. Performed and directed maintenance at Marine Corps Air Station Miramar and during two tours in Iraq (total time 15 months) to ensure mission safety and readiness for operations. Proved effective as short-term project leader directing multiple operation events and major maintenance projects under pressure.

SCHEDULING AND COORDINATION: Performed daily inspections on assigned aircraft; assisted in preflight inspections performing final checks; monitored aircraft performance during flight; assisted as a lookout and advised pilot of obstacles and other aircraft.

TECHNICAL SKILLS: As Helicopter Mechanic, performed inspection and maintenance duties on various aircraft systems, including the fuel, flight control, rotor, utility, and power plant systems; checked cockpit controls, switches, and safety devices.

CRITICAL THINKING AND PROBLEM SOLVING: Analyzed weight, mission, cargo and prepared aircraft for maximum defense. Utilized evaluative and technical skills in operating aircraft mounted weapons systems.

PLAN AND ORGANIZE WORK: Assisted in the supervision and administration of aircraft maintenance operations. Developed methods and procedures to improve efficiency of the Flight Crew, especially in flight operations or emergency maintenance procedures.

CUSTOMER SERVICES: Ensured safety for both passengers and cargo planning. Analyzed and loaded cargo efficiently to meet deployments and readiness planning.

TRAINING / COMMUNICATIONS: Using effective verbal and written communication skills, trained junior Marines in every aspect of the Marine Corps, including history, financial education, alcohol awareness, weapon safety, martial arts, tactics, and professional development.

KEY ACCOMPLISHMENTS:

LOGGED 1,200+ FLIGHT HOURS WITHOUT A SINGLE LOSS OF LIFE OR AIRCRAFT during two tours in Iraq and in the United States, including during combat conditions. Earned numerous recognitions, including Navy and Marine Corps Achievement Medal and numerous Air Medals. Participated in armed interdictions, border patrolling, medical evacuations of military and civilians, and special operations.

AS PLANE CAPTAIN, performed essential systems and safety checks for every aircraft under my care daily prior to operations (up to 14 helicopters). Led team effort in achieving a perfect safety record for my unit over 3.5 years and two combat tours. Trained junior staff in aircraft operations, aerial gunnery, combat tactics.

MILITARY TRAINING

- Naval Aviation Air Crewman Candidate School at NATTC, NAS Pensacola, FL.
- Survival, Evasion, Resistance, and Escape (SERE) School at Brunswick, ME.
- "A" and "C" school, CH-53E Crew Chief Training Syllabus at CNATT MAR Unit, MCAS New River, NC.
- "C" school, CH-53E Crew Chief Training Syllabus at CNATT MAR Unit, MCAS New River, NC.
- Plane Captain (PC) Ground syllabus for type aircraft.

EDUCATION:

January 2010, Bachelor of Arts, Government and Public Policy, cum laude. University of Baltimore, Maryland. Relevant Coursework: Constitutional Law; Bureaucracy and Public Policy; American Public Policy; Comparative Government; State and Local Government; Methods in Government and Public Policy; American Political Thought; Ethical Issues in Business and Society. GPA: 3.7 out of 4.0.

35 credits toward degree in International Marine Transportation, 09/2002-05/2003, New York Maritime College, Bronx, NY.

High School Diploma, 2002, Bethesda-Chevy Chase High School, Bethesda, MD.

AWARDS AND RECOGNITION

Navy/USMC Achievement Medal, 2007
2 Iraq Campaign Medals, 2007, 2004
16 Air Medals
USMC Good Conduct Medal, 2006
Global War on Terrorism Service Medal, 2004
National Defense Service Medal, 2003
Sea Service Deployment Ribbon
Certificate of Commendation
Certificate of Appreciation (2d Award)
Expert Rifle Badge
Expert Pistol Badge (2d Award)

OTHER INFORMATION:

Maryland Drivers License
Current Interim Top Secret Government clearance
Eagle Scout, Boy Scouts of America
CPR and First Aid Certified through the Red Cross

JEREMY D. DENTON
1234 Anywhere Street
City, State, Zipcode
Phone: 555.555.5555
Email: jeremy.d.denton@gmail.com

May 14, 2010

Government Printing Office
Human Capital Operations
732 North Capitol Street NW
Room A-638
Washington, DC 20401

Dear Ms. Howard:

Enclosed is my application responding to Vacancy Announcement # 10-346057-rm, Management and Program Analyst.

I have enclosed my federal resume, which highlights my professional accomplishments over the last decade.

I can offer the Office of Human Capital of the GPO proven Management and Program Analysis expertise, together with a Bachelor of Arts degree in Government and Public Policy, plus strong executive leadership experience in the following areas:

- **Critical Thinking, Analysis, and Problem-Solving** – Experienced short- and long-term project analyst, with field experience in using evaluative and technical skills to analyze and optimize operations quickly and decisively.
- **Work Planning, Organization, and Management** – Assisted in the supervision and administration of essential aircraft maintenance operations, including at remote, challenging locations. Developed methods and procedures to improve efficiency of the Flight Crew, especially in flight operations or emergency maintenance procedures.
- **Leadership** – 5 years with the US Marine Corps as a highly effective, successful, decorated sergeant and project leader able to direct multiple events under extreme pressure, including in combat situations.

I would like to have the opportunity to offer my extensive experience to the GPO Human Capital Office. I look forward to the opportunity to meet in person for an interview.

Thank you for your consideration of my application materials

Sincerely,

Jeremy D. Denton

Enclosures: Federal Resume

Military Status:
U.S. Air Force, E-5, 5 years experience
Aircraft Armament Systems Craftsman

VACANCY ANNOUNCEMENT

Defense Finance and Accounting Service
http://www.dfas.mil/careers/

Qualifications:
Applying for positions based on One Year Specialized Experience.
BS Degree in Accounting will be finished within months.
- **Accounting Technician, GS-0525**
- **Special Agent, GS-1811**
- **Target Federal Grade level: GS-5/7**
- **Salary range:** $38,790.00 - 50,431.00 USD /year

Career Change Duties/Keywords: These keywords are from the Accounting Technician job announcement. As an Armament Systems Craftsman, he actually does perform these accounting and data recording duties. He will require a second resume for the Special Agent application with different keywords and core competencies. He will still emphasize the Accounting background with the Special Agent federal resume. Each series above has a slightly different set of keywords. You can find keywords at *www.usajobs.gov* within each job announcement. Add these words into your resume.
- Maintains general ledger accounts, and reconciles electronic interfaces to general ledger from other systems.
- Reconciles subsidiary ledgers to control summary accounts.
- Posts inventory accounting transactions, property accounting transactions, and calculates and posts depreciation.
- Reviews and processes unusual or difficult accounting transactions ensuring the propriety and validity of supporting documentation, and determining the appropriate account and methodology for processing.
- Researches current accounts, historical data, source documents, etc., to develop and explain detailed information not otherwise readily available.
- Compiles, analyzes, and summarizes data from systems, documents, and reports.
- Identifies trends, discrepancies, and patterns for further analysis by accountants.
- Performs fiscal year-end review and close-out of accounts.
- Analyzes and prepares special reports on the causes of recurring adjustment actions; determines the cause of processing errors or problems and recommends corrective procedures.

QUALIFICATIONS REQUIRED:

One year of specialized experience equivalent in level of difficulty and responsibility to that of the next lower grade or pay band level within the federal service, which demonstrates the ability to perform the duties of the position, is required.

- **Specialized experience is defined as** reviewing and processing unusual or difficult accounting transactions, compiling, analyzing, and summarizing data from systems, documents, and reports, and determining the appropriate account and methodology for processing.
- Examples of Qualifying **Specialized Experience** include: Maintaining accounting or financial ledgers; posting financial transactions; preparing accounting reports; reconciling accounts and working with a variety of accounting systems.
- In addition to meeting the specialized experience requirements, applicants must describe how their experience meets the competencies within the body of the resume. **No separate statements addressing KSA's or competencies are required.**

Competencies:

- Knowledge of accounting concepts, principles, practices, procedures, and techniques.
- Skill in applying research techniques to gather information and analyze data.
- Proficient oral and writing communication skills to present clear and concise information.
- Ability to develop familiarity with the systems, practices, regulations, and operations using the specific procedures of automated systems to find and review accounting data in transaction files, ledgers, accounts, summary reports, and financial statements.

BERNIE THOMAS GANNON
Atlanta, GA 31645
Contact phone: (999) 888-8888
Contact email: jongannon@gmail.com

US Citizen
Social Security Number: 111-11-1111
Veterans Preference: 5 points, US Air Force, 06/2005 to present
Security Clearance: Secret (active)

WORK EXPERIENCE

06/2005 to present, AIRCRAFT ARMAMENT SYSTEMS CRAFTSMAN, E-5, US Air Force, various locations worldwide, 40+ hours per week, Lily Stewart, 222-222-2222, may contact.

PLAN AND ORGANIZE equipment maintenance activities for more than 3,000 pieces of maintenance safety and protection equipment, special purpose recoverables and alternate mission equipment valued in excess of $3.1 million. Deployed and supported ground forces in Operation Iraqi Freedom; met more than 980 combat missions on time.

ACCOUNT FOR AND ESTABLISH CONTROL to ensure maximum readiness. Interpret and implement military policy directives and instructions pertaining to maintenance, logistical supply and shipping of ground equipment, supplies and parts. Produce detailed Excel reports to demonstrate inventory, readiness and supply item availability.

LEAD TEAMS of up to five personnel performing a wide range of maintenance and related work. Provide technical assistance to complex problems. Prioritize and assign work. Monitor and assure quality of work; mentor team members. Prepare input to fitness evaluations.

RECEIVE, ISSUE AND STORE EQUIPMENT from flight line personnel; inspect and oversee repair; ensure readiness of all equipment and gear; distribute as appropriate and ensured accountability of all issued items, consistent with US Air Force and Department of Defense regulations, policies and procedures. Maintain PROPERTY BOOK to include transactions affecting accountability. Conduct periodic inventories, as required by regulations, of supplies and equipment items. Assign control numbers and log documents in control register.
IDENTIFY DISCREPANCIES AND PERFORM DAILY RECONCILIATIONS of critical assets. Prepare regular, detailed written reports of findings. Develop and update local procedures for effective inventory/property book functions to ensure accountability and maintain readiness.

PROVIDE TECHNICAL ADVICE, ASSISTANCE AND GUIDANCE on supply, maintenance and storage needs. Interpret complex blueprints, specifications, safety regulations and technical manuals. Identify, discuss and resolve technical issues. Interact daily with a wide range of internal and external customers, including senior level military officers. Maintain open communications; exercise tact and diplomacy on all occasions.

RESEARCH, DOCUMENT, ANALYZE AND INTERPRET military rules, regulations, standards and technical data, as well as Occupational Health and Safety Administration (OSHA) regulations. Ensure accurate and current written historical record of equipment. Review maintenance records; document inspection findings and recommendations. Analyze data to IDENTIFY INADEQUACIES, recommend corrective actions to prevent the development of possibly dangerous trends or weaknesses in maintenance and readiness processes. Use AUTOMATED SYSTEMS to monitor trends, analyze equipment and maintenance requirements, maintain equipment records and document maintenance actions. Summarize results; prepare and submit relevant reports to commanding officers.

ENSURE HAZARDOUS AND NON-HAZARDOUS MATERIALS ARE MAINTAINED AND STORED SAFELY in accordance with applicable regulations, inventory and records are maintained accurately and storage space utilized efficiently. Develop long-range equipment maintenance plans; ensure documentation is up to date and accurate; establish procedures to PREVENT WASTE, FRAUD, LOSS AND DAMAGE of maintenance supplies and equipment.

ANALYZE INVENTORY, MAINTENANCE RECORDS AND OTHER DATA; PREPARE DETAILED WRITTEN REPORTS AND RECOMMENDATIONS using Word, Excel and Outlook and specialized software including the Integrated Maintenance Data System, to track and monitor inventory, supplies, readiness of equipment and other related information. Ensure reports are accurate and timely. Analyze inventory reports, identify anomalies, resolve discrepancies. Research and prepare recurring and special written reports for commanding officers. Accurately forecast needs to meet anticipated requirements. Prepare standard operating procedures; analyze existing procedures and technical manuals; recommend changes to improve effectiveness.

COMMUNICATE DAILY WITH INTERNAL AND EXTERNAL CUSTOMERS. Train new airmen; prepared and deliver briefings to senior officers. Develop collaborative relationships with all levels of military personnel. Research and resolve complaints. Make recommendations to improve operations.

KEY ACCOMPLISHMENTS: Essential to BRAC success; conducted 100 percent inventory of 960 pieces of equipment; inventory completed 8 days early. Developed and implemented equipment sign in and out procedures; monitored 960 pieces with zero discrepancies. Deployed and supported ground forces in Operation Iraqi Freedom; met more than 980 combat missions on time.

07/2001 to 06/2003, ASSISTANT MANAGER, Hollywood Video, 105 S. Vista Road, Boise, ID 83708, 45 hrs per week, $7.50 per hour, Duff Bright, 222-222-2222, may contact.

EVALUATED EFFECTIVENESS OF OPERATIONS; identified deficiencies and developed plans to address. Monitored and tracked operations, ensured compliance with all applicable policies and procedures. Identified and reconciled any deficiencies, urgency interest and impact of the work. Leveraged resources to ensure timely, cost-efficient and effective operations.

DEMONSTRATED EXCEPTIONAL CUSTOMER SERVICE; interacted daily with a diverse range of personnel, from customers to colleagues to other managers. Assisted customers in identifying needs; make recommendations of products to meet those needs. Ensured customer satisfaction without compromising company policies or procedures. Demonstrated professionalism, courtesy and tact on all occasions, despite occasional provocation from customers and other stressful situations.

REVIEWED, ANALYZED AND RECONCILED INVENTORY; ensured product availability. Followed up on discrepancies and resolved problems.

ENGAGED IN PROACTIVE ORAL COMMUNICATIONS WITH A WIDE VARIETY OF INTERNAL AND EXTERNAL CUSTOMERS in order to provide information, advocate for new approaches and respond to a wide range of questions. Prepared and presented briefings, training and reports; ensured all presentations were appropriate for the target audience. Demonstrated professionalism, tact and courtesy on all occasions, even when under pressure or delivering negative information.

DIRECTLY SUPERVISED UP TO 15 TEAM MEMBERS; set work priorities and goals; mentored them to provide outstanding customer service and exceed organizational goals and objectives, offering advice and instruction as needed. Assisted in the overall planning, direction and timely execution of the store's operations. Assigned and evaluated work, with an eye toward continual improvements in efficiency and effectiveness. Ensured that employees were fully briefed on goals, strategies and policies.

PROMOTED TEAM APPROACH to problem solving and sales. Shared plans and information and sought input from colleagues and managers; built consensus to ensure optimal efficiency and effectiveness.

EDUCATION

2009 (expected), Bachelor of Science, University of Phoenix, Phoenix, AZ, major: accounting, 105 semester hours; 19 credits to be completed
Knowledge of accounting concepts, principles, practices, procedures, and techniques. Relevant coursework: Economics for Business, Financial Accounting I, Financial Accounting II, Corporate Finance, Contemporary Business Law I, Contemporary Business Law II, Intermediate Financial Accounting I, Intermediate Financial Accounting II, Intermediate Financial Accounting III, Advanced Financial Accounting, Computers and Information Processing

2002, Diploma, Jones High School, Irondale, AL

AWARDS AND RECOGNITION

AF Outstanding Unit Award, 2008
USAF NCO PME Graduate Ribbon, 2008
Iraq Campaign Medal, 2007
Global War on Terrorism Medal, 2007
Air Force Expeditionary Service Ribbon with Gold Border, 2007
Airman of the Quarter, 2006
National Defense Service Medal, 2006

PROFESSIONAL TRAINING

Airman Leadership School, 2009
2W171 Craftsmen Course, 2009

PROFESSIONAL PROFILE

Motivated, dedicated and detail oriented specialist with sound education in accounting and related underlying fields including accounting principles, finance, automated financial systems, and computers and information processing. Thirty hours of accounting and related fields.

Proven record of accomplishment for reconciling complex issues, analyzing, monitoring and tracking inventories, and producing reports using a variety of commercial and proprietary software programs. Proven analytical and information management skills.

Excellent written and oral communications skills. Recognized for providing excellent customer service to internal and external customers. Works well under pressure with multiple tasks. Polished, professional presentation. Fluent in Portuguese.

Bernie T. Gannon
1010 Edmondson Ave.
Atlanta, GA, 31645
(999) 888-8888
bgannon@resume-place.com
April 25, 2010

Federal Human Resources Recruiter
Defense Finance and Accounting Service
3333 Milton Ave.
Cleveland, OH, 90999

Dear Human Resources Recruiter:

Please find enclosed my federal resume, DD-214 and performance evaluation for the position of **Accounting Technician, GS-0515-7.**

My relevant qualifications include:
- Five years of experience as an Aircraft Armament Systems Craftsman. As a Craftsman, I have general competencies that will support my skill as an Accounting Technician.
- As an Armament Systems professional, I controlled supplies and maintenance equipment for maximum readiness and ensured safety of 3,000 pieces of equipment.
- As an analyst, I have researched discrepancies among inventory and property book products. I am skilled in reviewing, reports and statistics to determine effectiveness and efficiency of the program.

I would be an asset to your organization because:
- I have 5 years experience planning and organizing equipment maintenance for a significant operation in Europe and in multiple locations.
- My ability to lead teams of up to five professionals is proven. The team members maintain the equipment and provide technical assistance.
- I have proven my ability to study, learn, and write reports with my completion of my B.S. degree in Business with a major in accounting.
- I have been recognized for my skill in reconciling complex issues with inventory control for flight line personnel to ensure readiness of operations.

I would like to apply my accounting degree and experience to an entry-level position with DFAS, the largest accounting firm in the world. Thank you for your time and consideration.

Sincerely,

Bernie Gannon

Enclosures: Federal Resume, DD-214 and transcript

GETTING STARTED – FIND YOUR DOCUMENTS

Writing your first federal resume means finding your career documents, evaluations, past resumes, and other paperwork so that you can identify the dates of your assignments, training courses, and awards. This is critical to writing your first resume or federal resume.

ASSEMBLE YOUR CAREER DOCUMENTS AND BEGIN YOUR BASIC FEDERAL RESUME

- Separation papers
- DD-214
- Current Leave and Earnings Statement (LES)
- Performance appraisals
  - Coast Guard: Performance Reviews
  - Navy: Fitness Reports (Officers) or Performance Evaluations (Enlisted)
  - Army: Evaluation Reports (Officer, Non-Commissioned Officer or Enlisted)
  - Marine Corps: Fitness Reports (E-5 & above) or Proficiency Conduct Marks (E-4 & below)
  - Air Force: Officer Performance Evaluation Report or Enlisted Performance Appraisal
- DD-2586: Verification of Military Experience and Training (VMET)
- Military Training Record
  - -- Coast Guard: Educational Assessment Worksheet (CGI 1560/04e)
  - -- Navy: Electronic Training Record
  - -- Marine Corps: Basic Training Record (BTR)
  - -- Army: Education & Training Section of the OMPF
- Training certifications and forms
- Previous resumes or employment forms
- Award citations
- Letters of commendation and letters of appreciation
- Articles or letters concerning military activities
- Professional organization memberships or conference attendance materials
- College transcripts
- Military transcripts
  - Navy & Marine Corps: Sailor & Marine Transcript (SMART)
  - Army: Army/American Council on Education Registry Transcript (AARTS)
  - Air Force: Community College of the Air Force Transcript
- Course descriptions for courses relevant to your objective
- Specialized training (include joint or other training which may not be listed elsewhere)

OBTAINING YOUR VERIFICATION OF MILITARY EXPERIENCE AND TRAINING (VMET) DOCUMENT

To get your verification document, go to the VMET web site at http://www.dmdc.osd.mil/vmet. All separating military personnel can electronically download and print their VMET from the VMET Web site.

Follow the instructions and download your document. You can now get your verification document at any time online; however, you should retrieve it no later than 120 days prior to your separation. If you have problems getting your VMET and need assistance, check with your Transition Counselor.

... Once You Receive Your Verification Document

Identify the items that relate to the type of work or education you are pursuing and include them in your resume. If there are problems with information listed on the form, follow the guidance indicated below for your respective service:

- **Army:** Review and follow the guidance provided by the Frequently Asked Questions (FAQs) listed on the VMET online website.

- **Air Force:** Follow the instructions in the verification document cover letter or contact your Transition Counselor.

- **Navy:** Contact your Command Career Counselor or your local Fleet and Family Support Center Transition Office.

- **Marine Corps:** Follow the instructions in the verification document cover letter. If you need further assistance, contact your Administrative Office.

FEDERAL RESUME WRITING SECTION-BY-SECTION, BASED ON THE INSTRUCTIONS IN THE OPM'S OF-510

What to include in your federal resume

PERSONAL INFORMATION:

Full name, mailing address (with ZIP code), day and evening phone numbers (with area code), social security number, country of citizenship, veterans' preference, reinstatement eligibility, and highest federal civilian grade held.

Email: Sign up for an internet email address that includes your last name if you can, so that your email can be searchable.

Address: Some federal job announcements require that you live within a 50-mile radius of where the job is located, and others state that they will not pay for relocation. This is difficult to handle, because you cannot live in multiple locations while job hunting. Read the information about the location and "who can apply" carefully. If you see a job that's in the Washington, DC area and it requires that you live within a 50-mile radius, disclose in your resume that you are willing to relocate at your own expense, or that you have a military move coming to you.

Telephone: Cell phones are great for job searches because you can set up a professional voicemail and take most of the calls yourself (instead of family or co-workers). On the other hand, job interviews are not great on a cell phone!

Social Security Number: You must include your Social Security number (SSN) on your federal resume. The government securely manages employees and job applicants via the SSN number. If you do not include your SSN, you will not be considered for a job. It's as simple as that.

Country of Citizenship: Most federal jobs require U.S. Citizenship but some allow non-citizens with working visas to apply for jobs. Read the vacancy announcements.

Veterans' Preference or Veterans' Hiring Program: 5-Point Preference or 10-Point Preference, if eligible.

Reinstatement Eligibility and Highest Federal Civilian Grade Held: If you previously worked for the U.S. government as a civilian, include your highest job title and grade, and the dates held here.

JOB INFORMATION:

Announcement number, title, and grade.

Objective: This information can be added to the top of the resume, or you may simply include the title of the position, grade and announcement number in the agency's profile or registration pages when you set up your resume and information into the agency's database.

WORK EXPERIENCE CHRONOLOGY:

Job title, duties and accomplishments, employer's name and address, supervisor's name and phone number, starting and ending dates (month and year), hours per week, salary, and indicate whether or not your current supervisor may be contacted. Prepare a separate entry for each job.

Write details (duties, supervisors, phone numbers) about the last 10 years; write less information about positions prior to 10 years.

EDUCATION:

Colleges or universities, name, city and state, majors, and type and year of any degrees received (if no degree, show total credits earned and indicate whether semester or quarter hours). High school, name, city, and state, and date of diploma or GED.

OTHER QUALIFICATIONS:

Job-related training courses (title and year). Add classroom hours if more than 8 hours.

Job-related skills

This is an important section to add important keywords, skills, specialized qualifications, knowledge of systems and programs and other information that could help you to stand out when the supervisor reviews resumes.

COMMON QUESTIONS AND ANSWERS

WHAT DO SUPERVISORS CONSIDER WHEN MAKING SELECTIONS?

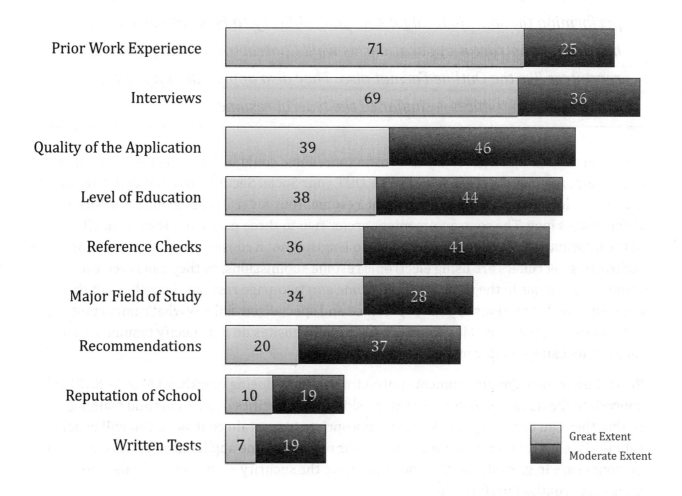

Category	Great Extent	Moderate Extent
Prior Work Experience	71	25
Interviews	69	36
Quality of the Application	39	46
Level of Education	38	44
Reference Checks	36	41
Major Field of Study	34	28
Recommendations	20	37
Reputation of School	10	19
Written Tests	7	19

Supervisors look closely at your Work Experience section of your resume to determine if you are qualified for the position.

WHAT IS THE DIFFERENCE BETWEEN A GOVERNMENT CONTRACTOR RESUME AND A FEDERAL RESUME?

The contractors who are working side-by-side with federal workers are performing the same federal jobs, so your Military to Federal Resume can be used for contractor applications as well! Contractor human resources recruiters like the Outline Format also. They also appreciate more details about your experiences -- similar to the federal resume.

The good news is that a government contractor resume could be basically the same resume as a federal resume, except that you TAKE OUT your Social Security number and veterans' preference information from the top of the resume. Your federal resume might be three to four pages long. The contractors might prefer two to three pages, but they want all of the information about your experience, so length is not a consideration. Government contracting recruiters are using electronic resume submissions, so they can receive a three-page resume in the same amount of time as a two-page resume. Length is not the question, the descriptions of your experience and specialized skills is what's important to the contracting recruiter. Most contractor resume websites do not specify resume length; they are focusing on relevant experience.

Recruiters from major government contractors, such as Boeing, Lockheed Martin, SAIC will appreciate the details of your experiences, skills, and specifics of locations and training, so that they can decide if your skills are appropriate for certain contracts. You will usually submit the electronic resume format into their online resume application systems. Military personnel are in great demand because you have the security clearances they need for immediate contract performance.

HOW DO I FIGURE OUT WHICH FEDERAL JOB TITLES MATCH MY MILITARY EXPERIENCE?

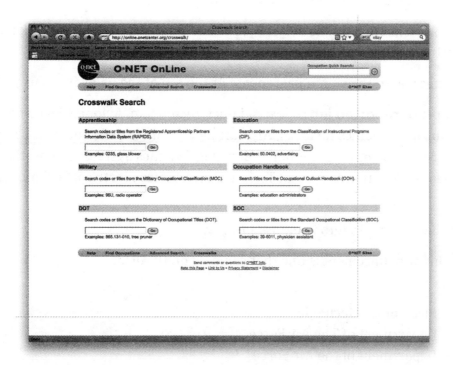

Trying to figure out which federal job titles will match up to your military experience can be a challenge, and many military to federal jobseekers are finding that a good place to start doing this is using the online tool provided by O*NET OnLine, a tool created for the U.S. Department of Labor, Employment & Training Administration.

How to Use O*NET:

1. Go to *http://online.onetcenter.org/crosswalk/*

2. In the box under the header "MILITARY" type your military job title.

3. You will get a list of possible military job titles. Pick one closely matching yours to get the summary report.

4. In summary report, at the top, you will see a paragraph titled "Sample of reported job titles."

5. Type these job titles into the search function at www.usajobs.gov to find vacancy announcements related to your military experience.

Example

- Go to *http://online.onetcenter.org/crosswalk/*, and under "Military" we typed in "Aviation Electronics Technician Second Class."

- You will see a list of possible related job titles. Find and click on the link for "49-2091.00 - Avionics Technicians."

- This brings you to the summary report. At the top of the page, find this paragraph:

    - **Sample of reported job titles:** Avionics Technician, Avionics Electronics Technician, Avionics Installer, Aircraft Electrical Systems Specialist, Aviation Electronics Technician, Avionics Manager, Avionics Systems Integration Specialist, Aviation Electrical Technician, Avionics Electrical Technician (AET), Avionics Tester

- Search these job titles into *www.usajobs.gov*.

- Today, this announcement is one that came up on USAJOBS:

Job Title: Electronics Mechanic
Department: Department of The Air Force
Agency: Department of the Air Force
Job Announcement Number: AFPC-334731-916077-9G-LRM

SALARY RANGE:	48,981.00 - 57,142.00 USD /year
OPEN PERIOD:	Tuesday, March 30, 2010, to Monday, April 05, 2010
SERIES & GRADE:	WG-2604-11
POSITION INFORMATION:	Full-Time, Multiple Appointment Types
PROMOTION POTENTIAL:	11
DUTY LOCATIONS:	1 vacancy - RAF Croughton, AE United Kindgom
WHO MAY BE CONSIDERED:	U.S. Citizens and Status Candidates

CHAPTER 2:
FOCUS YOUR FEDERAL RESUME IN THE OUTLINE FORMAT

Sell yourself with your accomplishments, keywords, projects, and specialized experience

FOCUS YOUR FEDERAL RESUME IN THE OUTLINE FORMAT

Writing your federal resume is one of the most important documents you may write in your career. The art and science of writing this resume is twofold: it must be written specifically toward the job you are seeking by studying the Duties and Qualifications sections of the vacancy announcement; the resume must be formatted for easy reading in the Outline Format. Central to this, of course, is applying for jobs that you are truly qualified for. If you achieve all this, you will have job interviews and offers!

This chapter will show you several ways to add specialized federal job description content, keywords, accomplishments, projects, and military training and awards that will achieve the results you are seeking.

FIVE WAYS TO FOCUS YOUR RESUME AND STAND OUT!

Look at the sample federal resumes in the Outline Format in this chapter and notice the keywords, military details, headlines, accomplishments, core competencies, and special electronic formatting solutions. These details are the key to an outstanding application!

1. Use keywords and language from the announcement.

2. Use the Outline Format with headlines.

3. Feature specific accomplishments

4. Write a comprehensive summary of qualifications at the top of your resume.

5. Learn electronic resume tips to create a first-rate database application.

LET'S LOOK MORE CLOSELY AT THESE FIVE IMPORTANT WRITING LESSONS FOR YOUR OUTLINE FORMAT FEDERAL RESUME

1. USE KEYWORDS AND LANGUAGE FROM THE ANNOUNCEMENT

These important keywords and content are located in the duties, qualifications, and other paragraphs of the announcement. As stated in the next chapter, *Understanding Federal Vacancy Announcements*, every resume sample in this book and CD-ROM will include important keywords and skills for the targeted job announcement. For many automated resume management systems, keywords and skills are integral to a successful application. Keywords are important for the Resumix resume systems, as well as for the HR Specialists who read resume descriptions to ensure qualifications for the job.

2. USE THE OUTLINE FORMAT WITH HEADLINES

The ALL CAPS HEADLINES make the resume easy to read by federal human resources specialists, and easy for you to write about five or six of your top skills (that are related to your next career). The Outline Format can summarize the number of "hats you wear at work," or your top skills that you use every day in your job. These ALL CAPS KEYWORDS will keep the reader engaged longer, and may result in further consideration of your application!

3. FEATURE SPECIFIC ACCOMPLISHMENTS

The Office of Personnel Management instructions for writing the federal resume (OF-510) state these two simple words for writing the Work Experience section of your resume: *Duties and Accomplishments*. The duties are covered with keywords and content. Include accomplishments in your resume to make it unique to you.

Your accomplishments speak directly to the hiring manager about your personal experiences. Hopefully, your words will impress hiring managers enough so that they will want to interview you and seriously consider you as an employee in their offices. Accomplishments demonstrate what you have DONE in the past and what you are CAPABLE of in the future.

Your accomplishments should be specific, such as projects with details, or specific results with supporting information to demonstrate specialized experience. When writing about your accomplishments, include project title, task name or situation, your actions, important challenges you overcame, and the results with supporting information.

4. **WRITE A COMPREHENSIVE SUMMARY OF QUALIFICATIONS**

A Summary of Qualifications is a synopsis of your most important career experiences. An abstract of approximately 350 words, it is your "elevator speech" on paper that will impress the reader with your highest-level experiences.

The best place to add this summary is at the top of your resume in a paper format federal resume. Some resume builders do not have a field for the summary, but others have. The Army has a resume builder in which you can copy and paste an entire resume into one online field. This is a convenient, flexible format. As of now, the space for a summary for Navy, USMC, and AF is the Summary of Qualifications at the end of the resume builder. You could also post the summary in the "Additional Information" field at the end of the USAJOBS builder.

Wherever you place the summary, it is an important resume section, because it is an excellent opportunity to engage the reader, highlight important keywords and skills, and unite your entire military career picture into a compelling, action-oriented paragraph.

Tips for writing an optimal Summary of Qualifications:

- Analyze the announcement "duties and qualifications" section.
- Write your summary based on the targeted knowledge, skills, abilities, and duties of the position sought.
- Include your leading skills and experiences.
- Strive to make your summary a "page-turner" introduction.
- Your goal is to impress the hiring official to want to meet you, set up an interview, and/or consider you for his or her team.

5. RESUME BUILDER TIPS

Do's & Don'ts for Resume Builders

DO -

DO - Compile & Research
- Locate all of your written career documents, such as resumes, evaluations, and position descriptions.
- Research keywords, skills, and industry language.
- Consider your experience, skills, and career interests.
- Determine your salary requirements and qualifications.
- Schedule time to research, write, and edit. Regard this as a career management project.

DO - Focus Your Resume Content
- Write one resume that will include keywords for one federal job / occupational series at a time.
- Emphasize the last 10 years of experience.
- Write your best attempt, then edit again – twice!
- Find an editor or additional person to review your resume.

DO - Include Your Accomplishments

- For each of your past jobs relevant to the position being sought, include one to three of your greatest accomplishments with details. Remember to make every effort to grab your reader's attention!

DO - Formatting and Readability
- IMPORTANT: Compose and edit your resume in a word processing program, then copy and paste your resume text into the online form or resume builder.
- Adhere to the page length instructions or character limitations for each agency.
  TIP: If you are writing a five-page resume, include your most recent information within the first three pages.
- Use easy-to-read type fonts, such as Times Roman or Arial.
- Use readable font sizes: 11 or 12 point type.
- Maintain at least one-inch margins around the copy.
- Use ALL CAPS and small paragraphs for the resume builder resumes.
- Insert white space to improve readability, such as a double space between paragraphs.

For a Paper Federal Resume:
- Use easy-to-read type fonts.
- Use readable font sizes.
- Maintain at least one-inch margins.

Remember your passwords and usernames.

Study, read, and follow the examples in this book and on the CD-ROM.

DON'T -

- Don't use oversize paragraphs (keep paragraph length approximately 4-8 lines).

- Don't write long-winded, run-on sentences. Keep sentence length concise and easy to read (7 to 14 words per sentence).

- Don't use third person verbs, for instance "directs and coordinates." Use present tense verbs for your current position, for example, "plan, direct, and coordinate." For past positions, use "planned, directed, and coordinated."

- Don't copy and paste your position description language or evaluations direct and uncut into your resume.

- Don't overuse acronyms; aim for as few as possible. If you do use acronyms, spell out the words followed by the acronym in parenthesis the first time you use it. Example: Department of Defense (DoD). Thereafter, you may use the acronym alone.

CASE STUDY 3

KEN SMITH
AVIATION ELECTRONICS TECHNICIAN SECOND CLASS
SEEKING ELECTRONICS TECHNICIAN, FV-F/G OR
INFORMATION TECHNOLOGY SPECIALIST, GS-5

Military Status:
Aviation Electronics Technician Second Class (5/06 – 4/10)
United States Navy (USN)

VACANCY ANNOUNCEMENT

Qualifications:
Applying for positions based on One Year Specialized Experience.
No college degree at this point. (44 credit hours)
- Electronics Technician, FV-0856-F/G
- Information Technology Specialist, GS-2210
- Target Grade: GS-5/7
- Salary Range: 35,000.00 - 63,400.00 USD /year

Duties/Keywords: These keywords are from the Electronics Technician for FAA job announcement. Each job series has a slightly different set of keywords. You can find keywords at *www.usajobs.gov* within each job announcement. Add these words into your resume in the work experience section.
- Install and maintain electronic equipment and lighting aids required for aviation navigation
- Assure a reliable, safe, and smooth flow of air traffic.
- Work with radar, communications, computers, navigational aids, airport lighting aids, and electrical/mechanical support
- Periodic maintenance (inspection and analysis of equipment with associated adjustments), corrective maintenance, troubleshooting, repair and replacement of malfunctioning equipment, and certification.
- Assist in the design, development and evaluation of new types of electronic equipment
- Travel throughout a large geographic region of the country
- Install new electronic equipment at a wide range of facilities and remote locations.

Qualifications Required: (also keywords for the resume)
Note: This applicant will qualify based on "one year specialized experience" for all of the above position.
A college degree is not required. This candidate could apply for a FV-F level because of his 4 years experience. Be sure to add examples of your qualifying experience into your federal resume.

Qualification Requirements: FV-F
Undergraduate and Graduate Education: Major study or at least 24 semester hours in any combination of the following: computer science, mathematics, electronics, physical sciences, information management, engineering, telecommunications, or other fields related to the position.
OR
3 years of work experience, 1 year which was equivalent to at least FV-E, that provided a basic knowledge of the principles of electronics, mathematics, computers, aeronautics, or related areas, or an understanding, both theoretical and practical, of automated systems operation, integration, management, and maintenance. Experience may have been gained in occupations such as computer specialist, electronics technician, telecommunications specialist, engineer, or other work related to the position to be filled.

FV-5%
1 year of specialized work experience with at least 1 year equivalent to at least the FV-F level that provided the opportunity to acquire and the need to apply practical and theoretical knowledge of the principles, functions, and processes associated with electronics and electricity concepts; computer systems and information management concepts telecommunications concepts; and system management and integration methods.

KEN SMITH
Louisville, KY 40272
Work: (502) 000-0000
John.smith@navy.mil
Social Security Number: xxx-xx-xxxx
Citizenship: U.S. Citizen
Veteran's Preference: 5-point preference, U.S. Navy Veteran, 2006-2010

WORK EXPERIENCE

AVIATION ELECTRONICS TECHNICIAN SECOND CLASS (5/06 – 4/10)
United States Navy (USN), Naval Air Station (NAS) Whidbey Island
3730 North Charles Porter Avenue, Oak Harbor WA 98278
Full-Time: 40+ hours/week
Base Salary: $36,082
Supervisor: Sunny Smith (360) 257-8872

SUPERVISOR: Supervised a team of 21 technicians in the repair and upkeep of sophisticated military electronics systems. Skilled Electronics Technician with 5 years of progressive experience performing and leading others in the maintenance and repair of sophisticated military electronics systems.

MAINTENANCE AND SERVICE OPERATIONS: Coordinated periodic maintenance and service activities with engineers and other cross-functional team members and conducted quality assurance inspections of all completed work. Have history of quick, accurate performance in the identification and resolution of complex issues affecting multiple systems.

TESTING EQUIPMENT: Used testing tools, including Multimeters, Megometers, Time Domain Reflectometers, and Oscilloscopes to ensure equipment adhered to the highest operational standards.

QUALIFIED IN INSPECTION AND REPAIR: Resident Expert in GPS, IRDS (Infrared Detection System), CRT/Flat Panel displays, Camera/Video Imaging systems, Single Board Computer equipment and many other military electronic systems. Also troubleshooting and repair of RS-232, IEEE 1388, and Ethernet Busses.

PROBLEM-SOLVING, ENGINEERING SCHEMATICS: Interpreted engineering schematics to identify and resolve system issues. Have history of quick, accurate performance in the identification and resolution of complex issues affecting multiple systems.

CONTRACTOR SUPPORT AND PROCUREMENT: Interfaced with external contractors and vendors to procure equipment and services.

INSTRUCTOR: Conducted training sessions for as many as 80 technicians covering all required shop qualifications. Able to create, lead, and direct training for large groups of technicians. Train and utilizes safety practices and procedures following established safety rules and regulations and maintains a safe and clean work environment.

LICENSED GROUND SUPPORT EQUIPMENT OPERATOR

KEY ACCOMPLISHMENTS:

SYSTEMS RELOCATION: Led a 15-person team tasked to relocate over $10M in military electronics systems. Completed the staging, packing, and unpacking of over 100K lbs of components and supplies to meet critical mission timelines (2009).

QUALITY ASSURANCE: Demonstrated consistent track record of upgrading/repairing military electronic components in record time, resulting in substantial minimization in hardware downtime.

SYSTEM UPGRADES: Spearheaded significant rebuild of critical electronics system, identifying and leading team in the replacement/repair of several mission critical components (2008).

EDUCATION
Undergraduate Studies, Sullivan University, Louisville, KY 40214; 44 semester hours completed toward Bachelor's Degree in Information Technology, 2007. Certificate of completion for prerequisite Microsoft courses for the MCSE. GPA: 4.0.

High School, Seminole High School, Seminole, FL 33776, 2004.

PROFESSIONAL TRAINING
Microsoft Windows Vista, Configuration, Training Camp, 120 hours, 2009
Windows Server 2008 Active Directory, Configuration, Training Camp, 120 hours, 2009
Windows Server 2008 Applications Infrastructure, Configuration, Training Camp, 120 hours, 2009
Windows Server 2008 Network Infrastructure, Configuration, Training Camp, 120 hours, 2009
Enterprise Support Technician, Training Camp, 120 hours, 2009
Enterprise Administrator, Training Camp, 120 hours, 2009
Avionics Common Core, NATTC Pensacola, FL, 30 weeks, 2007
Connector and Wire Repair, NAS Whidbey Island, WA, 30 weeks, 2007
Aviation Electronic Technician O-Level, NATTC Pensacola, FL, 24 weeks, 2007
Electronics Theory/Fundamentals, NAS Whidbey Island, WA, 16 weeks, 2006
P-3C Avionics, NAS Whidbey Island, WA, 20 weeks, 2006
Server Administrator, Training Camp, 120 hours, 2006

COMPUTER SKILLS:

Platforms: Microsoft Windows 2000, XP 32/64, Vista 32/64, Server 2003/2008, Apple OS XS

Systems Software: Active Directory, Domain Name Service (DNS), Windows Software Update Services (WSUS), Internet Information Services (IIS), Host-Based Security System (HBSS), VMware, Acronis Backup & Recovery

Information Security: McAfee VirusScan, McAfee ePolicy Orchestrator (ePO), Host Intrusion Prevention Software (HIPS), Symantec Enterprise Secure

Web/Content Management: Joomla (CMS), WordPress (CMS)

Database: SQL Server, MS Access

Messaging: Navy Regional Enterprise Messaging System (NREMS)

Desktop: Microsoft Office Suite (Word, Excel, PowerPoint), MS Visio, Virtual PC, Diskeeper, APC Powerchute, FileMaker Pro, Symantec Ghost, Symantec Antivirus Suite

CERTIFICATION AND LICENCES

Aviation Electronics, United States Navy, Oak Harbor, WA (2007)

General Radiotelephone Operator License with Ship Radar Endorsement, Federal Communications Commission (FCC)

AWARDS/ACHIEVEMENTS

Global War on Terrorism Service Medal

Navy and Marine Corps Achievement Medal

Navy Good Conduct Medal, USN

National Defense Service Medal

Sea Service Deployment Ribbon-3, USN

Armed Forces Expeditionary Medal

Global War on Terrorism Expeditionary Medal

SKILLS SUMMARY

Highly skilled, professionally Electronics Technician with significant experience in electronics and information technology support for military and civilian clients. Combines technical project leadership with hands-on expertise in developing, managing, and maintaining sophisticated military electronics systems and government-owned/operated LANs. Proven ability to handle complex responsibilities in a demanding work environment.

CLEARANCE Top Secret (current)

KEN SMITH
1234 Anywhere Street
Louisville, KY 40272
Phone: 555.555.5555
Email: kensmith@gmail.com

May 20, 2010

Mike Monroney Aeronautical Center
HQ, Room 156 (AMH-140)
6500 South MacArthur Blvd.
Oklahoma City, Oklahoma 73169
Attention: Toshia Hill
Phone: 405-954-7949
Email: latoshia.hill@faa.gov

Dear Ms. Hill:

Enclosed is my application responding to **Vacancy Announcement # ASW-FS-10-273-122392, Electronics Technician, FV-0856-F/G.**

I have served in the U.S. Navy as an Aviation Electronics Technician Second Class for the past five years.

My specialized expertise includes five years experience as:
* Military Electronics Technician, Instructor, and Supervisor with complex military electronics equipment.
* Skilled with utilizing schematic diagrams and test equipment in maintenance and service operations.
* Train and direct technicians in testing, troubleshooting, and repairing electronic equipment.
* Supervisor and designer of quality assurance techniques and instruction methods to ensure safe, efficient, and accurate performance and troubleshooting.
* Qualified in inspection and repair. Resident expert in multiple electronic systems.

I have proven that I am a team leader who works very well within an organizational unit to support activities that ensure the safe and efficient repair and operation of Navy ships. I would like to provide the same work ethic and technical expertise to FAA's aircraft and electronics systems.

I am available for a rotating shift, as well as domestic and international travel, in support of FAA aircraft. I would like the opportunity to provide quality and safety electronics technical services for the FAA in Ft. Worth, TX.

Thank you for your consideration.

Sincerely,

Ken Smith

Attachments: Federal Resume, DD214

Military Status:
Army National Guard

VACANCY ANNOUNCEMENT

Qualifications:
Applying for positions based on One Year Specialized Experience.
BS in Business
- **Administrative Officer (GS-0301)**
- **Management and Program Analyst (GS-0304)**
- Salary range: $ 47,448.00 - 74,628.00 USD /year
- Target grade: GS 9/11

Duties/Keywords: These keywords are from the Administrative Officer job announcement. The Management Analyst keywords are similar, but emphasize analysis more than administration. Each series above has a slightly different set of keywords. You can find keywords at *www. usajobs.gov* within each job announcement. Add these words into your resume.
- Full staff assistant to the Executive Office
- Coordinate administrative matters
- Interpret administrative policies; developing and implementing local policies
- Define administrative requirements
- Provide advice to Executive Management on related issues
- Track inquiries and required reports
- Coordinate responses
- Establish and maintain a file system/system of records
- Tracking/update new service level agreements
- Lead on special project initiatives and/or process improvements
- Ability and knowledge to access and is skilled in the use of databases
- Locate and retrieve data to validate reports and provide responses to routine inquiries

Qualifications Required: (also keywords for the resume)
GS-09 Specialized Experience:
One (1) full year of specialized experience, which equipped the applicant with the particular knowledge, skills, and abilities to perform successfully the duties of the Administrative Officer, GS-09 position, and that is typically in or related to the work of the position to be filled. Specialized experience includes: 1) knowledge performing **evaluative studies to identify, consider, and resolve changing administrative issues;** 2) Knowledge of **administrative laws,** regulations, policies, and precedents; 3) knowledge in **analytical and evaluative methods** and techniques to improve the efficiency and effectiveness of program operations of regional organization in addition to substantive program administration functions. NOTE: Evidence of specialized experience must be supported by detailed documentation of duties performed in positions held. Please provide such documentation on resume.

MARILYN LOGAN
Baltimore, MD 21228
Email: Marilyn.logan@gmail.com

US Citizen
Social Security Number: 222-22-2222
Veteran's Preference: 5 points, Army National Guard of the United States, Active Duty
08/2006 to 08/2010
Security Clearance: Secret

WORK HISTORY

09/2007 to 08/2010, READINESS NON-COMMISSIONED OFFICER, E-7/SFC, 40 hours per week, Salary: $5,640 per month, U.S. Army National Guard, CO B 581th MSB, 79 Mellor Ave., Catonsville, MD 21228, MSG Pierre Holmes, 410-333-3333, Contact: yes.

SENIOR ADVISOR AND ADMINISTERED mobilization readiness program to support unit personnel in preparation for changing deployment requirements. Advised Commander on training, logistics, personnel and overall readiness requirements, ensuring compliance to Army regulations. Knowledgeable of administrative policies, procedures and processes. Continually improved administrative processes to meet changing demand for personnel and workflow.

MANAGED ANALYTICAL AND EVALUATIVE STUDIES. Analyzed data and prepared reports for senior leadership. Coordinated personnel and administrative actions for soldiers. Oversaw and monitored Military Occupational Specialty qualification program for unit personnel. Planned and coordinated Family Readiness Group activities to assist deployed soldiers and their dependents.

SUPERVISED AND LED activities of unit support staff and logistics personnel. Ensured missions were performed by qualified personnel within allowed time and according to established policies and procedures. Assigned tasks, monitored activities, and conducted performance evaluations for subordinates.

USED AUTOMATED SYSTEMS TO DEVELOP, TRACK AND REPORT Battalion information. Collected data, prepared and submitted monthly drill and annual training payrolls. Scheduled soldier's training in automated Army training system. Developed and stored operational and personnel correspondence and documentation. Generated and presented reports to Battalion Headquarters.

DEVELOPED, WROTE, AND EDITED correspondence, reports, and other documents, ensuring accuracy of content, style and grammar. Researched and located information in complex databases. Collected information on soldier status and strength; prepared weekly reports and presented findings to commander and higher headquarters for review and approval. Prepared and reviewed training directives, schedules and records, mobilization plans, Standard Operating Procedures, and unit readiness and unit status reports.

ACCOMPLISHMENTS: Instrumental in preparing 60+ soldiers for deployment in support of Operation Iraqi Freedom. Initiated Family Readiness Group to support over 60 deployed personnel and their dependents; coordinated distribution of care packages to deployed soldiers. Assisted in coordination of deployment of 200 personnel and equipment in support of Operation Enduring Freedom; coordinated pre-deployment convoys to move unit's vehicles to deployment site. Planned and conducted training for 200 personnel.

05/2006 to 09/2007, PROPERTY BOOK NON-COMMISSIONED OFFICER, E-6/ SSG, 40 hours per week, Salary: $4,040 monthly, Maryland National Guard, 4848 Reisterstown Rd., Reisterstown, MD 21228, MSG Apollo Williams, 410-444-4444, Contact: yes.

REVIEWED REQUESTS FOR, LOCATED, AND TRANSFERRED required equipment and gear for mobilizing units preparing for deployment, ensuring equipment readiness. Ensured accountability of all issued items, consistent with U.S. Army and Department of Defense regulations, policies and procedures.

COMMUNICATED AND INTERACTED with Area Support Group personnel to facilitate efficient and timely equipment transfers and inventory maintenance. Maintained contact and exchanged information with unit personnel regarding the monitoring of hand receipt validation, property transactions and inventory reconciliation.

USED AUTOMATED SYSTEMS, DATABASES AND COMPUTER APPLICATIONS to efficiently perform duties. Developed documentation to support equipment transfers and inventory levels. Monitored unit hand receipts and performed monthly updates using automated Standard PROPERTY BOOK System-Redesign. Prepared and generated unit reports for five battalions within Area Support Group. Verified unit equipment on hand in database, ensuring match to monthly Unit Equipment Readiness List.

CONDUCTED AND MONITORED INVENTORIES, as required by regulations, of supplies and equipment items. Maintained PROPERTY BOOK for units to include transactions affecting accountability. Identified discrepancies and performed daily reconciliations of critical assets. Prepared regular, detailed written reports of findings and presented to Property Book Officer; reports included recommendations for improving operations.

GATHERED AND ANALYZED PERTINENT PROGRAM DATA, FORMED CONCLUSIONS, DEVELOPED REPORTS AND MADE RECOMMENDATIONS. Analyzed data on excess and shortage items; developed reports with recommendations for cross-leveling of excess equipment among units to improve overall readiness.

ACCOMPLISHMENTS: Located available equipment and prepared documentation for equipment transfers for mobilizing units.

11/2005 to 05/2006, TRAINING NCO/ADMIN/LOG SUPPORT, E-6/SSG, 40 hours per week, Salary: $3,717 monthly, Maryland National Guard, 1008 Transportation Company, 1818 Reisterstown Road, Reisterstown, MD, SFC Buddy Cramer, 410-444-4444, Contact: yes.

ADMINISTERED AND MANAGED COMMANDER'S TRAINING AND MOBILIZATION READINESS PROGRAM in support of mission objectives. Prepared and submitted forecasts for individual training requirements to higher headquarters to ensure seat allocation. Maintained mobilization and training records, and managed training library. Read and interpreted Army regulations to determine appropriate course of action for all training and readiness activities; advised leadership on all initiatives.

SUPERVISED AND LED activities of unit support staff, supply sergeant and training non-commissioned officers. Assisted in planning and coordinating missions assigned by higher headquarters. Ensured missions were performed by qualified personnel within the time constraints allowed, with zero accidents or injuries. Assigned tasks, monitored activities and conducted performance evaluations and counseling for subordinates.

USED AUTOMATED COMPUTER SYSTEMS TO DEVELOP, STORE, TRACK AND REPORT Battalion information. Collected data, prepared and submitted monthly drill and annual training payrolls. Entered submission of personnel for military occupational specialty and professional development schools into automated Army Training Requirements Reporting System. Generated and presented reports to unit Commander.

DEVELOPED, WROTE, AND EDITED various reports and other documents. Reviewed training directives and assisted in developing unit's monthly training schedules and annual training plans. Developed unit status reports and monthly drill payroll.

ACCOMPLISHMENTS: Assisted in preparing 40+ unit personnel for deployment in support of Operation Iraqi Freedom. While working at Soldier Readiness Processing site, led team to process hundreds of personnel actions and meet deadlines for required daily processing. Assumed unit operations when Readiness Non-commissioned Officer was transferred. Assisted in planning and coordination of Battalion diversity fair; supervised two stations. Started Enlisted Promotion Systems program to fill vacancies in the unit; assisted recruiter with events to attract new soldiers.

EDUCATION

2000, Bachelor's Degree, University of Ohio, Dayton, Ohio, Major: Business Administration (27 hours in business courses), GPA, 3.27 out of 4.0.

PROFESSIONAL TRAINING

Army Ethics Training, 2006; Equal Opportunity Representative, 2005; Family Readiness, 2004; Advanced Noncommissioned Officer Course, 2003; Motor Transport Operator ANCOC, 2003; Active Guard Reserve Initial Entry Training Program, 2002; Technical Transportation of Hazardous Materials (AMMO 62), 2002; Defense Demilitarization Program, 2001; Standard Army Maintenance System 2 Sustainment, 2000; Basic Noncommissioned Officer Course, 1995;

AWARDS, HONORS, RECOGNITION

Global War on Terrorism Service Medal, 2006
Army Reserve Component Achievement Medal
National Defense Service Medal
Armed Forces Reserve Medal
Non-Commissioned Officer Professional Development Ribbon 3rd Award
Army Service Ribbon
Armed Forces Reserve Medal with M Device

MILITARY SERVICE

Army National Guard of the United States (ARNGUS), 08/2006 to 08/2010, Honorable Discharge

PROFESSIONAL PROFILE

Talented leader and advisor with ability to analyze, interpret and implement complex rules and regulations and make prompt decisions. Notable success in developing, administering and managing successful programs to facilitate mission accomplishment. Proven track record for meeting targets and exceeding goals. Excellent communications skills, including proficiency at preparing correspondence and reports, and superior ability to communicate with individuals at all levels. Goal oriented, high energy individual with excellent attention to detail. Knowledge of government laws and regulations in regards to acquisition of services and supplies. Willing to relocate.

MARILYN LOGAN
1111 Mystery Lane
Baltimore, MD 21228
Email: Marilyn.logan@gmail.com

May 20, 2010

Detroit DEU
Denver HRC
Phone: (313)596-7213
Email: hrmdeu@va.gov

Re: Job Announcement Number: VB347790--MB, Administrative Officer
Department Of Veterans Affairs, Veterans Benefits Administration

Dear VBA Human Resources Recruiters:

Enclosed is my application for Administrative Officer.

I have served in the National Guard as an Operations Manager with specialization in administration, property, training, and readiness for the past five years.

My specialized expertise includes:
- Leading evaluative studies to support changing Guard requirements for readiness, materials, and administration.
- Knowledge of and skill in analytical and evaluative methods to improve efficiency and effectiveness of the Guard program operations.
- Proven administrative officer capabilities, including report generation, tracking information, and records management.
- Ability to communicate with senior officers, customers, and team members to achieve operations objectives.
- Efficient computer skills, including data management, spreadsheet development, and efficient report development.

I would like the opportunity to provide my administrative, analytical, and communications skills to the Veterans Benefits Administration. I am highly efficient and focused on customer services for the veterans.

My team leadership skills can be utilized at VBA to improve services and disability claims management and the administration to support these critical operations..

Thank you for your consideration.

Sincerely,

Marilyn Logan

Attachments: Federal Resume, DD214

Military Status:
U.S. Coast Guard, E-5, 3 years experience
Gunner's Mate, Small Arms Instructor

VACANCY ANNOUNCEMENT

Qualifications:
Applying for positions based on One Year Specialized Experience.
No college degree at this point. (23 credit hours)
- **Transportation Security Officer (TSO) (SV-1802-D/D) - TSA**
- **Police Officer (GS-0083) – Any Law Enforcement Agency**
- **Background Investigator (GS-1810) – OPM, Many agencies**
- **Security Assistant (GS-0086) – Many agencies**
- **Target Grade level: GS-5 or D/D (TSA pay band)**
- **Salary range:** 32,318.00 - 48,477.00 USD /year

Duties/Keywords: These keywords are from the Patrol Officer job announcement. Each series above has a slightly different set of keywords. You can find keywords at *www.usajobs.gov* within each job announcement. Add these words into your resume.
- Protect property and persons
- Enforces appropriate criminal codes and regulations
- Issues traffic citations and federal violation notices when necessary.
- Responds to crowd and riot control, bomb threats and search requests.
- Questions witnesses and principals in crimes reported on VA property.
- Investigate crimes and arrest persons for offenses committed
- Patrol in the outlying grounds
- Directs and assists persons to safety areas during fire, storm or other emergencies
- Takes prompt action to evacuate persons from dangerous areas.

Qualifications Required: (also keywords for the resume)
Note: This applicant will qualify based on "one year specialized experience" for all of the above position.
A college degree is not required. This candidate could apply for a GS 7 position also for any of the above positions. Be sure to add examples of your qualifying experience into your federal resume.
GS-5 Level: Must have at least one year of specialized experience at or above the GS-4 grade level or the equivalent in the private sector. This experience must have provided knowledge of a body of basic laws and regulations, law enforcement operations, practices, and techniques and involved responsibility for maintaining order and protecting life and property. Examples of qualifying experience: work on a police force; service as a military police officer; work providing visitor protection and law enforcement in parks, forests, or other natural resource or recreational environments; criminal investigative duties.

BRANDON B. BILLINGS
394 Aalapapa Drive, Kailua, HI 96734
Cell: (808) 222-3333

WORK HISTORY

August 2007 to Present; U.S. Coast Guard, BOARDING TEAM MEMBER / SMALL ARMS INSTRUCTOR (Gunner's Mate, E-5); Sector WaterWays Management and Security, Vessel Boarding Security Team, Honolulu, HI 96801; Supervisor: LT Bernie Watkins, (777) 333-3333; may contact.

SECURITY OFFICER / CONDUCT HARBOR PATROL. Conduct harbor security patrols in emergency response vehicles of Honolulu commercial harbors, Barbers Point, Kewalo Basin, Ala Wai, and Kaneohe Bay harbors. Maintain patrol logs of vessel activities within the harbor. Conduct Homeland Security boardings of all vessels entering Honolulu and Barbers Point harbors. Assist persons in distress and ensure security around waterways.

LAW ENFORCEMENT AND INVESTIGATION. Cooperate with and assist federal and state law enforcement officers in detection of criminals, such as smugglers or illegal entrants. Investigate suspicious vessels and establishments in and around harbor areas. Participate in mutual law enforcement patrols with State Department of Land and Natural Resources. Inspect conditions of vessels and crews in compliance with and using knowledge of U.S. Coast Guard standards.

COMMAND INTELLIGENCE OFFICER. Log suspicious activities and send information to senior management for review and distribution to appropriate federal and state agencies.

FIRE ARMS INSTRUCTOR. Instruct in the teaching handling, operation, and maintenance of small arms weapons, ammunition, and pyrotechnics, including the use of the 9 mm Beretta, M16 A1 rifle, and riot shotgun. Maintain all ordnance / gunnery equipment, including mechanical, electrical, and hydraulic.

July 2006 to August 2007; DECKHAND (E-1 to E-4); U.S. Coast Guard, Cutter ACUSHNET; Honolulu, HI 96801; Supervisor: CDR Kenny Wilson, (777) 444-4444; may contact.

SAFETY AND SECURITY WATCH TEAM MEMBER. Enforced nation's laws and rescued people in trouble on waterways. Conducted search and rescue operations. Inspected ships of all sizes, from smallest watercraft to largest tankers to ensure seaworthiness and compliance with U.S. laws. Used advanced electronics, telecommunications, and computer systems.

DAMAGE CONTROL OFFICER / MAINTENANCE AND EMERGENCY REPAIR SPECIALIST. Maintained watertight integrity of Coast Guard vessels and emergency equipment used for firefighting and flooding. Performed plumbing repairs and welding fabrication and repairs. Inspected vessels for chemical, biological, and nuclear warfare. Trained in decontamination procedures. Assigned to engineering department and qualified to stand engineering watches.

EDUCATION

Albany Community College, Albany, NY; 23 quarter hours; 2004-2005
Albany High School, Albany, NY; Diploma; 2003

PROFESSIONAL TRAINING

Force Protection Fundamentals, Ship Board Security Engagement Weapons
Incident Response to Terrorist Bombings Awareness, Small Arms Instructor
Damage Control Personal Qualifications Standards
Intelligence Photography Course
Life Saving Equipment Manager
First Responder Awareness
Hazardous Materials
Gunner's Mate "A" School; Yorktown Virginia: Trained in electronics and mechanical systems and with hydraulics; 10 weeks; 2001

PROFESSIONAL LICENSE
Captain's License – 50 ton

COMPUTER PROFICIENCIES: Microsoft Word, Excel, Access, PowerPoint, Internet

Brandon Billings
304 Aalapapa Drive / Kailua, HI, 96734
(808) 222-2222
Brandon.billings@gmail.com
May 10, 2010

John Green, Human Resources Recruiter
Transportation Security Agency
7888 Leesburg Pike
Leesburg, VA, 20202

Dear Mr. Green:

Please find enclosed my federal resume for the position of Police Officer, GS-0083, Announcement #10101.

My relevant qualifications include:
- Three years specialized experience in security officer and harbor patrol with the U.S. Coast Guard as a Boarding Team Member.
- I have also served as a Firearms Instructor for new hires in the handling of arms, ammunition, and pyrotechnic equipment.
- My experience includes law enforcement and investigation of cases, such as smugglers and illegal entrants.

I would be an asset to your organization because:
- I have one year specialized experience in law enforcement operation practices and techniques.
- I can offer you experience in working as a member of a military police officer with extensive experience in visitor protection and law enforcement in the harbors and bays.
- I have experience in criminal investigative case development.
- My training in Microsoft and skill in writing reports will be an asset as a Police Officer and investigative agent.

Thank you for your time and consideration. I look forward to your response

Sincerely,

Brandon Billings

Enclosures
Federal resume, DD-214

CHAPTER 3:

UNDERSTANDING FEDERAL VACANCY ANNOUNCEMENTS

Learn how to analyze federal job announcements for mission, qualifications, and keywords

LEARN HOW TO UNDERSTAND AND ANALYZE FEDERAL JOB VACANCY ANNOUNCEMENTS

Researching and analyzing federal vacancy announcements is important for two reasons: the first is to locate significant federal job opportunities; the second is to identify keywords to include in your resume. When you are ready to focus your resume, you will return to the vacancy announcement and add keywords from the "duties" and "qualifications" sections.

Before you can find the best vacancy announcements for your skills and interests, it is helpful to understand what is in the vacancy announcement that is important to your job search. At first glance, federal job announcements seem lengthy and arduous to read. Take the time, however, to glean the information the federal human resources staff is conveying. *My experience has shown that when jobseekers become more familiar with vacancy announcements and "how to apply" instructions, they apply more frequently for jobs.* In this step you will gain understanding of federal vacancy announcements and the information you need to be a competitive jobseeker.

TWO TYPES OF JOB ANNOUNCEMENTS

Job Announcements with Specific Closing Dates: These announcements are for positions that are being specifically recruited for. The timing for responses could be as little as a couple of days or as long as several weeks. Agencies set these deadlines based on their experience with the relevant job markets.

Open Inventory / Standing Registers / Database Announcements: These are announcements for jobs that are continually being recruited for or when a future need is anticipated. The closing date could be the distant future, usually in one year. The names of qualified applicants are stored in a database, and HR staff will search the database when a supervisor requests a person meeting the job's requirements. Timing for filling jobs covered by this kind of announcement is unknown, so you may be in for a long wait if you respond to one. What is certain is that if you do not have your resume in the database, you won't be considered at all.

HOW TO READ AND UNDERSTAND
A FEDERAL JOB VACANCY ANNOUNCEMENT

Let's look at one vacancy announcement for the most important features of information that will affect your job search. We will use a Homeland Security Department, Customs and Border Patrol announcement for MISSION SUPPORT SPECIALIST (TRAINING) for our analysis.

Job Title: Mission Support Specialist
Department: Department Of Homeland Security
Agency: Customs and Border Protection
Job Announcement Number: MHCBPDE-286679-OC

SALARY RANGE:	40,949.00 - 64,403.00 USD /year
OPEN PERIOD:	Tuesday, September 22, 2009
	to Tuesday, September 21, 2010
SERIES & GRADE:	GS-0301-09/11
POSITION INFORMATION:	Full TimeCareer/Career Conditional
PROMOTION POTENTIAL:	11
DUTY LOCATIONS:	Many vacancies - Throughout the Nation
WHO MAY BE CONSIDERED:	United States Citizens

Title of Job: Mission Support Specialist

Series and Grade: This is a GS-0301-09/11. You can start in this position as a GS 9 or 11, or at various steps within GS 9 and GS 11.

Geographic Location: Many locations, be sure to check off your favorite locations. **WHERE WILL POSITIONS BE FILLED UNDER THIS ANNOUNCEMENT?** Positions will be filled at multiple locations throughout the United States and Puerto Rico. See list below to view the list of locations. You will be asked to identify your location preferences in the on-line application process. You may select no more than five duty locations. Once you accept or decline a job offer you will not receive further consideration under this announcement unless you re-apply. You can only have one application pending at a time for this announcement. If you re-apply, only your most recent application will be considered.

Who can apply: All US Citizens, which would include Veterans and Status applicants.

Closing date: This is an Open Inventory announcement, open for one year. The HR specialists will be search for applicants as they require new hires.

This is an open continuous announcement which will establish an inventory of applicants interested in a career as a Mission Support Specialist with U.S. Customs and Border Protection. This applicant inventory will be used to fill vacancies as they occur within the Office of Border Patrol at various locations throughout the U.S. and Puerto Rico.

DUTIES

As a Mission Support Specialist for the Department of Homeland Security, Customs and Border Protection, you will coordinate and perform a wide range of administrative and management services essential to the operation of the office (including, but not limited to, management and information systems, telecommunications, budget, finance, procurement, human resources, training, logistics, property, space, records and files, printing and graphics, mail, travel, and office equipment) and serve as an advisor to management on assigned administrative matters. In addition, you will conduct or participate in the evaluation of administrative programs, systems and methods, and identify ways to improve the efficiency and effectiveness of these services at the local level. You will also represent the office in dealing with vendors and organizations within the agency that have primary responsibility for these services

KEYWORDS TO ADD INTO YOUR RESUME FROM THE DUTIES SECTION:

- administrative and management services
- management and information systems, telecommunications, budget, finance, procurement, human resources, training, logistics, property, space, records and files, printing and graphics, mail, travel, and office equipment)
- advisor to management
- evaluation of administrative programs, systems and methods
- identify ways to improve the efficiency and effectiveness
- represent the office in dealing with vendors and organizations

QUALIFICATIONS AND EVALUATIONS (KEYWORDS IN BOLD)

GS-9: You qualify at the GS-9 level if you possess one year of specialized experience that equipped you with the skills needed to perform the job duties. This experience must have been equivalent to at least the GS-7 grade level. Examples include providing **assistance to senior specialists in the evaluation and analysis of operational and administrative programs to identify quantitative and qualitative productivity standards,** measures of performance and **reporting procedures, and resource utilization effectiveness and efficiency; assisting in the execution of** administrative programs by carrying out specified portions or segments of specific **projects** such as updating **budget** data on **spreadsheets,** preparing routine budget requests, preparing requests for **personnel action,** providing **orientation to new employees,** coordinating office moves and telephone service requirements, monitoring usage of government motor vehicles, and **collecting and analyzing information** related to workflow, office **procedures** and **control systems** in support of program evaluations; and identifying and recommending solutions to **administrative problems** and providing **advice** to staff on established methods and procedures.

KEYWORDS TO ADD TO YOUR RESUME:

GS-9: You qualify at the GS-9 level if you possess one year of specialized experience

- **assistance to senior specialists in the evaluation and analysis of operational and administrative programs to identify quantitative and qualitative productivity standards,**

- measures of performance and **reporting procedures, and resource utilization effectiveness and efficiency;**

- **assisting in the execution of** administrative programs by carrying out specified portions or segments of specific **projects**

- updating **budget** data on **spreadsheets,**

- preparing routine budget requests, preparing requests for **personnel action,**

- providing **orientation to new employees,**

- coordinating office moves and telephone service requirements

- monitoring usage of government motor vehicles, and

- **collecting and analyzing information** related to workflow

- office **procedures** and **control systems** in support of program evaluations
- identifying and recommending solutions to
- **administrative problems** and providing **advice** to staff on established methods and procedures.

HOW YOU WILL BE EVALUATED

You will be evaluated based upon the resume/transcript (if applicable) and responses you provide on the job specific questionnaire that is required as part of the application process for this position. The automated system will assign you a self-assessment score based on your responses to the on-line questionnaire. You will be assigned a score ranging from 70 to 100 points.

HOW TO APPLY

You will be required to complete the assessment questionnaire and upload your documentation in the system called Application Manager. Initially, the Application Manager requires you to create an account. Once your account is created, Application Manager provides a site where you can track the status of jobs you have applied to at Customs and Border Protection; upload documentation; view/print copies of notification letters; or print a copy of your questionnaire.

TO FAX A RESUME OR SUPPORTING DOCUMENTS:

If you previously uploaded documents to this vacancy, **please do not fax the same documents.** If you need to fax a part of your documentation:

- Click on the link below to obtain the special application cover page. http://staffing.opm. gov/pdf/usascover.pdf
- Make sure that you include the 8-character vacancy identification number LN286679. Provide your SSN, name, and address in the blocks provided or we will not be able to associate your document(s) with the rest of your application. Print your SSN and name neatly using the exact name as the one used when you filled out the assessment questionnaire. The fax number is **1-478-757-3144.**

ASSESSMENT QUESTIONNAIRE

Here are two sample Application Manager questions from this announcement.

Section 1   **Total Questions in this Assessment: 20**

1. Which of the following best represents your level of experience in conducting program evaluations?

> A I have had no experience in program evaluation.
>
> B I have assisted others with aspects of program evaluations.
>
> C I have led individual parts of a program evaluation.
>
> D I have been in charge of an entire program evaluation.
>
> E I have conducted numerous program evaluations.

2. Indicate the extent of your experience in developing an office's annual mission support plans.

> A I have had no experience in this area.
>
> B I have assisted with the development of an annual mission support plan.
>
> C I have managed the development of an annual mission support plan.
>
> D I have been on a committee that developed an annual mission support plan.
>
> E I have been solely responsible for the development of an annual mission support plan.

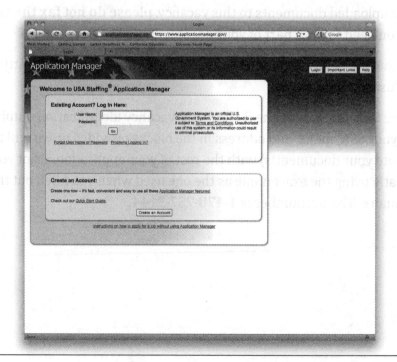

FINDING KEYWORDS AND SKILLS
IN THE VACANCY ANNOUNCEMENT:

Once you have found a vacancy announcement and read through it sufficiently to determine your interest and eligibility, it is time to analyze the announcement for keywords. This step is crucial! Without identifying the keywords, you cannot customize your application materials to the announcement. This is where you will market yourself to the human resources personnel and help them understand why you should be hired for the job.

Highlight the important skills and duties in the announcement. Read both the "duties" and the "qualifications" sections. Look at the following announcement samples and the words that are highlighted. If you can include these words (or some of them) in your resume as skills or experience, your package will stand out when the HR staff member reviews the applications. These two announcements have a wide range of grade level and salary offerings so that there is room for advancement. Training is expected and experience will be gained in the lower grades. You can enter these positions at any of the grades listed. These announcements with multiple grade offerings are a good source for positions offering career opportunity in government.

FIND YOUR KEYWORDS FROM YOUR VACANCY ANNOUNCEMENT:

Keywords from Example 1 – Intelligence Specialist

These words can become the ALL CAPS HEADINGS in the Outline Format

- Intelligence budget, manpower and personnel management
- Technical advice, review, evaluate and present briefings
- Briefings on manpower, personnel and budget requirements
- Program budget
- Resource programming
- Manpower program
- Intelligence organizational structures
- Technical advice / guidance
- Conduct studies
- Coordinate with staff to identify/recommend solutions

EXAMPLE 1 – DEPARTMENT OF THE ARMY

INTELLIGENCE SPECIALIST (OPERATIONS SUPPORT), JOINT ACTIVITIES	
Additional Duty Location Info: 1 vacancy - FL - Miami	
SALARY RANGE: 41,563.00 - 78,355.00 USD per year	**OPEN PERIOD:** Monday, July 18, 2010 to Monday, August 01, 2010
SERIES & GRADE: GG-0132-9/12	**POSITION INFORMATION:** - This is a Permanent position. -- Full Time
PROMOTION POTENTIAL: 11/12	**DUTY LOCATIONS:** 1 vacancy - FL - Miami
WHO MAY BE CONSIDERED:	
Applications will be accepted from United States citizens and nationals.	

MAJOR DUTIES:
You will be the Intelligence Directorates focal point for **intelligence budget, manpower and personnel management.**

Provide **technical advice, review, evaluate, coordinate, develop and present briefings on manpower, personnel & budget requirements, allocations and authorizations.**

You will develop/manage the **program budget**; prepare/submit intelligence initiatives and resource input.

Assess the adequacy of **resource programming** and recommend solutions.

Administer the **manpower program**; analyze **intelligence organizational structures**, functional alignments, command relationships, manpower requirements, utilization, and position grade structure requirements.

Provide technical advice/guidance;

Conduct studies of intelligence mission/workload changes involving multi-disciplined intelligence missions, functions & organizations.

Coordinate with the **staff to identify/recommend solutions** to unusual personnel related issues. This position requires knowledge of the **Intelligence disciplines and analysis**.

About the Position: The incumbent will work for the Director of the Plans Division, at Headquarters, United States Southern Command (USSOUTHCOM) in the Intelligence Directorate, Plans Division in Miami, Florida with normal working conditions and atmosphere. We are located in building 8401, NW 53rd Terrace, Miami, Florida.

EXAMPLE 2 – FEDERAL BUREAU OF INVESTIGATION

INVESTIGATIVE SUPPORT SPECIALIST GS 1801-5/7/9/11 (EX)

SALARY RANGE: 24,431.00 - 65,371.00 USD per year	**OPEN PERIOD:** Thursday, July 14, 2010 to Wednesday, July 27, 2010
SERIES & GRADE: GS-1801-05/11	**POSITION INFORMATION:** Excepted Service Appointment This position will be filled on a full-time, permanent basis.
	DUTY LOCATIONS: 1 vacancy - Houston, TX

WHO MAY BE CONSIDERED:

This announcement is open to all qualified applicants who reside within the Houston, Texas commuting area.

This position is being advertised concurrently under Merit Promotion procedures in Announcement Number HO-2005-0072. Candidates who wish to be considered under both External and Merit Promotion procedures must apply to both announcements. This position is also being advertised concurrently to FBI employees in all locations under Announcement Number HO-2005-0073.

JOB SUMMARY:

The FBI is like no other career choice you've explored. It's challenging, compelling, and important. Whatever your background or expertise, you will find an FBI future exceptionally rewarding because the work you perform will have a daily impact on the nation's security and the quality-of-life for all U.S. citizens.

Location: Houston, Texas

Working Hours: 8:15 - a.m. - 5:00 p.m.

Salary:
GS-5: $24,431.00 $35,657.00
GS-7: $33,979.00 $44,176.00
GS-9: $41,563.00 $54,028.00
GS-11: $50,287.00 $65,371.00

Relocation Expenses will be borne by the selectee, except employees returning from Legat assignment.

Area Information: Houston is the fourth largest city in the United States, with a population of 3.4 million people, and is the ninth largest field office in the FBI. Houston offers moderately priced housing, and numerous cultural and intellectual opportunities. There is no state income tax in Texas, and economic indicators are positive.

EXAMPLE 2 – (CONTINUED)

KEY REQUIREMENTS:

- U.S. Citizenship Required.
- The selectee must be able to obtain a Top Secret clearance.

MAJOR DUTIES:

GS 7:   Provides **essential investigative support** towards the Bureau's overall **investigative mission** by processing a variety of criminal and general (i.e. security, applicant, civil, etc.) investigative leads and portions of conventional investigative cases, barring any known or suspected indication of physical danger.

Receives assignments in terms of investigative leads and segments of more routine investigative cases emanating from officially assigned cases assigned to Special Agent personnel.

Utilizes manual and automated information resources, determine most viable sources of information and conducts research of varied information.

Prepares synopsis of research findings in proper format to be included for use in official investigative case documentation findings.

Prepares routine subpoenas and participates in personally serving same to individuals identified. Receives and/or participates in handling telephonic and face-to-face complaints from outside sources and the general public.

GS 9: Provides <u>vital</u> **investigative support** towards the Bureau's overall investigative mission by processing a full range and variety of criminal and general (i.e. security, applicant, civil, etc.) investigative leads and cases from inception to completion, barring any known indication of serious physical danger.

Responsible for **serving subpoenas**, maintaining and developing a wide range of diverse liaison contacts and sources.

Independently determines **necessary principal and supplemental leads** for research and analysis. **Receives general investigative cases,** being assigned as the "case Agent", to process from inception to completion.

Prepares graphic aids regarding research findings, such as assessments of property boundaries. Prepares detailed synopsis of research findings in final form to represent or supplement official investigative case document results.

Orally or in writing, sets out additional leads for coverage by other field offices and/or FBIHQ and/or advises case agent personnel of suggested investigative trails.

Initiates and prepares subpoenas, personally serves majority of these subpoenas.

EXAMPLE 2 – (CONTINUED)

MAJOR DUTIES (CONTINUED):

Prepares graphic aids regarding research findings, such as assessments of property boundaries. Prepares detailed synopsis of research findings in final form to represent or supplement official investigative case document results.

Orally or in writing, sets out additional leads for coverage by other field offices and/or FBIHQ and/or advises case agent personnel of suggested investigative trails.

Initiates and prepares subpoenas, personally serves majority of these subpoenas.

Provides significant advice and guidance to Agent personnel requiring subpoena(s) issued in connection with on-going cases.

On recurring rotational basis, handles telephonic and face-to-face complaints from outside sources and the general public. May be called upon to **testify** in a court of law as to content of information obtained manner of obtainment, and chain of custody of evidence.

Keywords for GS 7/9 from Example 2 – Investigative Support Specialist

- Investigative support for investigative mission

- Investigative leads

- Utilize manual and automated information resources

- Prepare synopsis of research findings

- Prepare routine subpoenas

- Vital investigative support

- Serve subpoenas

- Principal and supplemental leads for research

- Receive general investigative cases / case agent

- Prepare graphic aids

- Orally or in writing, advise on additional leads

- Give significant advice and guidance to Agent

- Testify in court

CHAPTER 4:

SEARCH FOR FEDERAL JOBS

Introduction to federal job listings, websites, and search techniques

MAJOR JOB SEARCH SITES AND ADVANCED SEARCH TECHNIQUES

Now that you better understand vacancy announcements, can interpret salary or grade information, and have collected a few target job titles, you may begin your search for suitable jobs on USAJOBS and other agency websites.

This chapter will give you a quick guide on how federal job search sites are set up, as well as an in-depth look at a range of popular job sites. These include independent agency websites and commercial automated systems used to recruit job candidates.

USAJOBS
Department of Navy Civilian Hiring and Recruitment Tool (DONHR)
U.S. Army Civilian Personnel Online (CPOL)

For a more comprehensive list of federal employment websites and databases, refer to the Quick Guide on the next page.

IMPORTANT "HOW TO APPLY" JOB TIP FOR FEDERAL JOBS:

Applying for federal jobs on any of the websites in this chapter or any agency will probably involve two to four steps for on-line applications. Each agency announcement will have different instructions, but they are basically these:

1. Complete a profile or registration on-line
2. Copy and paste your resume in their resume builder or form
3. You could be required to answer questions, submit narrative essays, or fill out a Supplemental Data Sheet
4. You might find instructions to fax DD 214, transcripts and other documents. Watch the timeframe for faxing!

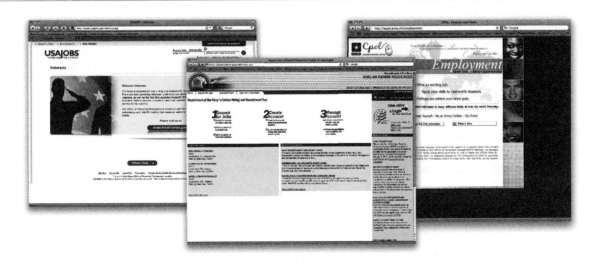

QUICK GUIDE

TO THE MOST POPULAR FEDERAL JOB LISTING WEBSITES FOR FORMER MILITARY PERSONNEL

www.usajobs.gov

The official Office of Personnel Management's website of federal job listings. You can create an individual profile to receive vacancy announcements by email. BEWARE: If you only use the email announcement system with specific job titles, you could be missing some jobs with titles that are new or unusual. It's best to search USAJOBS once per week, as well as sign up for the email service.

www.americajobs.com

A commercial website where you can read vacancy announcements and, for a small fee, sign up for an email service that will send you full vacancy announcements based on your criteria.

www.avuecentral.com

A commercial website with as many job listings as USAJOBS. You may submit your resume into their resume builder and apply for jobs at approximately 15 agencies, including FEMA, civilian U.S. Coast Guard, and Department of Homeland Security.

www.fedjobs.com

A commercial website where you can read vacancy announcements and, for a small fee, sign up for an email service that will send you full vacancy announcements based on your criteria.

SELECTED AGENCY WEBSITES WHERE AGENCY JOB ANNOUNCEMENTS, REGISTRATION, PROFILE, RESUME BUILDER, SUPPLEMENTAL STATEMENTS AND/OR SPECIFIC JOB-RELATED QUESTIONS MAY BE FOUND:

Civilian Army positions:	*www.cpol.army.mil*
Civilian Navy and Marines positions:	*www.donhr.navy.mil*
Air Force Personnel Center:	*www.afpc.randolph.af.mil/*
U.S. Coast Guard	*www.uscg.mil/civilian/*
Defense Logistics Agency:	*www.dla.mil*
Federal Bureau of Investigation:	*www.fbijobs.com*
National Security Agency:	*www.nsa.gov*
Central Intelligence Agency:	*www.cia.gov*

SEARCH THE WEBSITES OF EXCEPTED SERVICE DEPARTMENTS AND AGENCIES AND INTERNATIONAL ORGANIZATIONS

The following agencies do not always list their jobs on USAJOBS. Since they are not part of the competitive service, they are not required to list all of their jobs or internships on OPM's website. If you are interested in these agencies, you should look directly on their websites.

GENERAL AGENCIES:

Federal Reserve System, Board of Governors	Central Intelligence Agency
Defense Intelligence Agency	U.S. Department of State
Federal Bureau of Investigation	Government Accountability Office
Agency for International Development	National Security Agency
U.S. Nuclear Regulatory Commission	Post Rates Commission
Postal Service	Tennessee Valley Authority
United States Mission to the United Nations	

DEPARTMENT OF VETERANS AFFAIRS, Health Services and Research Administration:
Physicians, Dentists, Nurses, Nurse Anesthetists, Physicians' Assistants, Podiatrists, Optometrists, Expanded-function Dental Auxiliaries, Occupational Therapists, Pharmacists, Licensed Practical/Vocational Nurses, Physical Therapists and Certified/Registered Respiratory Therapists.

JUDICIAL BRANCH

LEGISLATIVE BRANCH

PUBLIC INTERNATIONAL ORGANIZATIONS:

International Monetary Fund	Pan American Health Organization
United Nations Children's Fund	United Nations Development Program
United Nations Institute	United Nations Population Fund
United Nations Secretariat	World Bank, IFC and MIGA

USAJOBS
One of the five most popular career job sites on the internet!

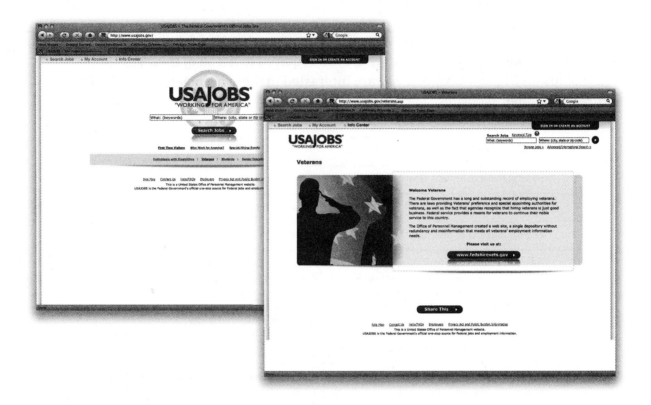

WWW.USAJOBS.GOV

To find vacancy announcements for jobs for which you are qualified or would be interested in, we recommended three search techniques involving just three to four criteria selections. Most likely, this will produce many interesting results.

SEARCH TECHNIQUE 1 – GEOGRAPHIC

1. Start at *www.usajobs.gov* and select the SEARCH link

2. Geographic Search – the entire state where you live

3. Agencies – SELECT ALL

4. Job Title - SELECT ALL

5. Click on YES if you have been in the military, or click NO to read announcements that are open to people who have not worked in government before.

All of the jobs in your selected state or city will appear. Scroll through them carefully as they may not be in alphabetical order. There will be a variety of jobs, grade levels, and titles. If you are qualified for a GS-7/9, you may scroll directly to these positions. Consider all job titles; a government job title doesn't tell the whole story!

SEARCH TECHNIQUE 2 – AGENCY

1. From the *www.usajobs.gov* home page, again select the *Advanced/International* link

2. Agency Search - SELECT AN AGENCY

3. Locations - SELECT ALL

4. Jobs - SELECT ALL

5. Click on YES if you have been in military or government, or click on NO if not.

For example, a search for all National Institutes of Health jobs, U.S.-wide, will display all available jobs nationwide. This type of search provides the broadest variety of job titles within the agency that you can find. Scroll through them all, even if there are 10 screens. Look for the grade level that is right for you.

SEARCH TECHNIQUE 3 – JOB TITLE

1. From the *www.usajobs.gov* home page, again select the *Advanced/International* link

2. Job title – SELECT A SPECIFIC TITLE

3. Location - SELECT GEOGRAPHIC LOCATION

DONHR – U.S. NAVY HUMAN RESOURCES
U.S. Navy Civilian Hiring and Recruitment Tool

The U.S. Navy and Marine Corps have their own website on which you can post your resume. You may copy and paste your resume into their online builder, then search for announcements that match your qualifications. Go to the "Jobs, Jobs, Jobs" page to search for civilian job vacancies by geographic area, salary, or job title.

NOTE: DON announcements are not particularly descriptive. They may have "generic" job descriptions instead of specific "duties," like other announcements. These are "Open Inventory" or database announcements.

HTTPS://CHART.DONHR.NAVY.MIL

Agencies Served	U.S. Navy and U.S. Marines
Announcements	Generic – short descriptions of duties
Closing Dates	Current listings and Open Inventory (mostly)
Resume Builder	8 Screens, copy and paste
Job Duties Length	6,000 characters
Registration / Profile	Questions Yes
Supplemental Data Sheet	Yes
How to Apply	Self-Nominate after resume is in database
Track & Follow-up	Not easy, no automated system

CPOL - U.S. ARMY CIVILIAN PERSONNEL ON-LINE
The Army Civilian Resume Builder and ANSWER Tool

Although the U.S. Army posts its civilian vacancies on the USAJOBS website, if you would like to be considered for a civilian position at any Army duty location, you MUST locate the vacancy announcements in CPOL and post your resume into the Army's resume builder. If you are interested in civilian positions with the U.S. Army, you might save time by going directly to this website to find the announcements and apply for the jobs.

(Applicant Notification System Web-Enabled Response)

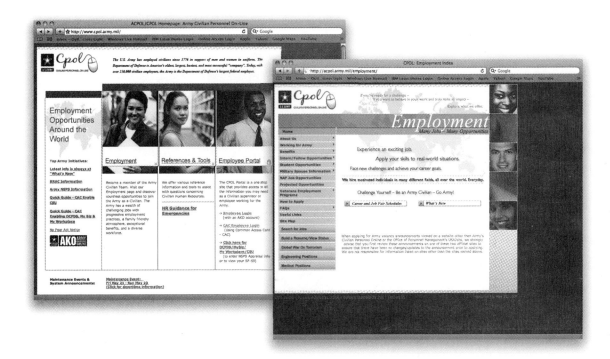

WWW.CPOL.ARMY.MIL AND HTTP://ACPOL.ARMY.MIL/EMPLOYMENT/

Agencies Served	U.S. Army military bases and agencies worldwide
Announcements	Both descriptive and generic
Closing Dates	Current listings and Open Inventory
Resume Builder	EXCELLENT – one field – copy and paste!
Registration / Profile	Questions Yes
Supplemental Data Sheet	Yes
Job-Specific Questions	No
Track & Follow-up	ANSWER system – track your job offers in a great database

CHAPTER 5:

APPLY FOR JOBS AND TRACK & FOLLOW-UP

How to submit your electronic or paper military federal resume to agency databases

SUBMIT YOUR ELECTRONIC OR PAPER MILITARY FEDERAL RESUME TO AGENCY DATABASES

Applying for any federal job calls for successful accomplishment of the 3 P's – patience, persistence and perspiration! Finding the optimal vacancy announcements for your experience, geographic location, and salary preference takes research and time.

You could conceivably find several jobs to apply for each week. With an average of 17,000 jobs listed every day, you could spend 10 hours per week researching the announcements, tweaking your resume, copying and pasting your resume into the various online builders, and tracking and following up on applications. It's a CAMPAIGN!

Federal Job Applications Are Different

The federal job search culture is different from private sector. The job titles are diverse, the resumes are distinct, there are often essay questions you must answer, there are terms that only the government uses, and the search may take months. At first glance this can be intimidating. Novice federal jobseekers might try to use materials they have prepared for the private sector, but they won't get far. Worse yet, some might give up or not even try. That's a shame, because once you learn how government hires, it's really not so difficult after all.

The reason the federal job search process is so complex is that your application package represents an examination (with scoring) of your qualifications. Think about it. In the private sector you submit a cover letter, a bare-bones resume, and perhaps a form or two. Hopefully, you're called in for a screening interview. After that, you might get called back for another one or two interviews that progressively delve deeper into your experience and qualifications.

The federal job application process involves presenting more about yourself up front: you may be required to answer job-related questions in your profile or registration; you submit a 2-4 page electronic federal resume; and, you often answer multiple-choice questions and write essays to specific questions. Only then—if at all—do you get to an interview. This way, the federal government can hire the best qualified people because they are the applicants who made it through the system.

Consider the movement of your resume through the federal human resources specialist's hands to the supervisor. Look at the chart on the next page:

FEDERAL HIRING TRAIL – WHAT HAPPENS TO YOUR RESUME

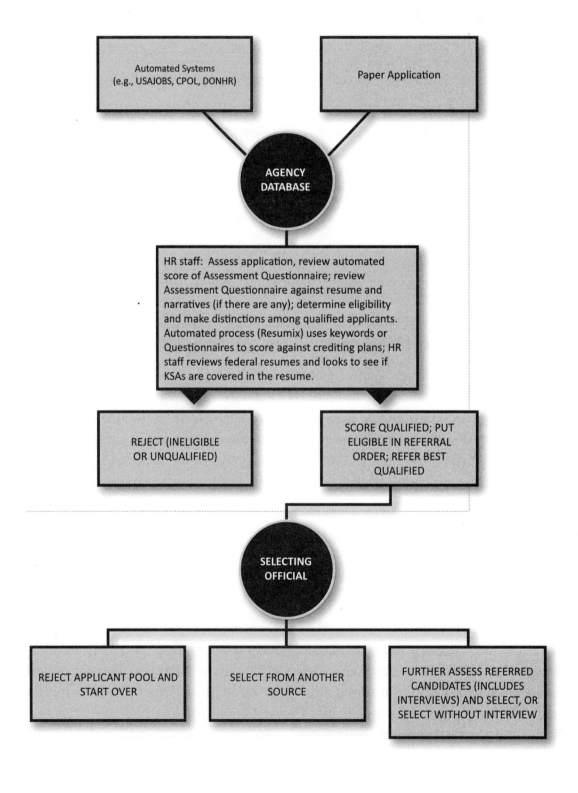

THE MOST IMPORTANT THING YOU NEED TO KNOW IS...

FOLLOW THE DIRECTIONS! Never deviate from the written instructions for any reason.

1. KNOW THE DEADLINE

Applications for federal job vacancies will only be accepted while the vacancy is "open" (the exception is for 10-point veterans). Open periods can be as short as a few days or as long as several weeks. They are set by the agencies and represent your window for applying for the job. The closing date is the last day applications will be accepted. It should be clearly indicated on the announcement.

You shouldn't leave your application to the last minute. If you do, be aware that the time of day on the closing day might be important. Many vacancy announcements, especially those on web-based systems, close at midnight on the closing date. Be mindful of how the deadline is expressed. The database for one of the systems many agencies use is maintained in Alexandria, VA, and the closing time is usually expressed in terms of Eastern Time (Standard or Daylight Savings).

2. PACKAGE WHAT THEY WANT – FOLLOW THE DIRECTIONS

Online Applications: For electronic applications, complete all of the pages and questions. Make sure you complete the submission. Sometimes there are at least three steps to applying: Profile / Registration; Resume Builder or Resume Submission; Questions or Essays. Be sure you are not exceeding the maximum number of characters allowed in a web box. There's very little formatting that you can do within web boxes, but make entries as easy to read as possible.

Combination online and fax or mail: If you are asked to apply online, but then fax or mail additional information, make sure you include your SSN, name, and announcement number on each paper submitted by mail or fax. You could add a cover letter to the package.

USAJOBS is continually improving vacancy announcement instructions and language. Along with other improvements to the format of vacancy announcements, their instructions continue to improve. Currently, you have to read each vacancy announcement very carefully, because important information is not presented in a uniform place or manner. The overall goal is to make vacancy announcements more user-friendly and to reduce the chance that applicants will make mistakes. But even after improvements are made to the announcements, the process will still be complicated and vary among agencies.

Set up your Accounts, Profile and Federal Resume in all or some of these automated federal job recruitment systems:

USAJOBS
www.USAJOBS.gov
OPM's Official Job Announcement and Application Site – Set up your Account here right away. USAJOBS includes announcements and the resume builder. Most of the positions with Air Force are posted with USAJOBS and applicationmanager.gov now.

Application Manager
www.applicationmanager.gov
This is the Assessment Questionnaire site used by USAJOBS. These two sites work together for federal resume and questionnaire. This is a popular combination. Set up your account here to begin your federal job search.

AvueCentral
www.avuecentral.com
About 20 federal agencies use this site instead of USAJOBS, but the announcements are still posted on USAJOBS. Set up your account if you want to apply to any federal jobs managed by avuecentral.com. Agencies that use Avue include: US Marshal's Service, Forest Service, Peace Corps, Library of Congress, Architect of the Capitol, Dept. of Justice (Justice Management Office), and about 20 other federal agencies. With Avue, you use their resume builder, their assessment questionnaire and attach files at this site.

CPOL
www.CPOL.army.mil
This is the official site for Army civilian jobs (but the announcements are still posted on USAJOBS. If you want to apply for Army civilian jobs, you MUST set up an account here.

DONHR
https://chart.donhr.navy.mil
This is the official site for all Navy and USMC jobs (but job announcements are also posted on USAJOBS. If you want to apply for Navy and Marine Corps civilian jobs, you MUST set up an account here.

Federal Resume & Assessment Questionnaire Applications

Many agencies are using a combination of the federal resume in USAJOBS and the Assessment Questionnaire from Application Manager. A defining characteristic is that they rely on multiple-choice and "yes-no" questions to make distinct among job candidates.

Application Manager (managed by USAStaffing / OPM)

This system is currently used by about 100 agencies. You will complete a profile, including copying and pasting your resume into one online field; answer more registration questions; then answer more job-related questions which are yes/no and multiple choice. In many instances your answer will trigger a box in which you will be asked to provide a short essay explaining your answer or demonstrating what experience, education, or training you have to support the answer you gave.

COPY AND PASTE KEYBOARD SHORTCUTS

You will need to get faster with copying and pasting your template resume into the agency resume builders. Try these keyboard shortcuts:

Control A – Creates edited copy
Control C – Copy
Control V – Paste
Control Z – If you loose something, you can type Control Z right away and get the copy back.

Resumix with keyword systems:

Resumix™ (Owned by Hotjobs.com)

This is the only knowledge-based keyword system used by government agencies. This system is used by NASA and all components of the Department of Defense (including Army, Air Force, and Navy). You submit a resume (called a "resumix" now because of this system) into a complex resume builder, answer personnel questions in a Supplemental Data Sheet, and then self-nominate for specific vacancies. A major distinction between Resumix™ and the question-driven systems is that Resumix™ does not use a series of questions to assess your qualifications. Instead, it applies artificial intelligence to read resumes and distinguishes among applicants through words and phrases included in their resumes.

Resume Tip: Use your electronic resume for the resume builders you will find on the individual Defense agency websites.

---

3. TRACK AND FOLLOW-UP ON APPLICATIONS

After you have submitted your resumes into the various databases, you CAN track and follow-up with many agencies.

Yes, you can. Asking questions, getting information, developing relationships, and getting known are all critical factors in standing out and getting hired. You can track and follow-up on most of your application for federal jobs. Not all, but most. Some of the on-line application systems are extremely automated and are set up so that you will be contacted.

Most vacancy announcements typically include the name of a human resources person who is responsible for many aspects of the announcement, including collecting the applications. This HR person might have created the vacancy announcement, posted it on USAJOBs and other websites, and communicated frequently with the hiring supervisor. They have knowledge of the application process, have the required information needed, and will soon be accepting all of the applications. They will then coordinate the review of the packages and be part of the rating and ranking process to determine who will get an interview. This HR person is important to you and your future with that agency.

Warning, they are busy!

The HR staff members are busy with multiple announcements, various aspects of announcement development, reviewing packages, and responding to supervisor needs. Use diplomacy and consideration when contacting them about your package. Your goal is to be helped and remembered favorably!

Play the Application Game

The best philosophy here is to learn all that you can about the jobs and internships that are excellent for your degree, experience, location, salary, and interests. Apply for as many of these applications and internships as you can find. Manage your campaign with dates and editing the packages to focus it slightly. In about 60 days, you will be receiving "hits." The sheer volume of your effort and energy will pay off. Make sure your paper federal resume or electronic version is written with the skills and keywords of your target jobs!

HOW CAN YOU CONTACT THE HR PERSON?
RECOMMENDED TELEPHONE SCRIPTS AND EMAIL MESSAGES:

Communicating by telephone: The HR person probably won't answer the phone, but they are there. They screen their calls. Be ready with a good voicemail. Practice your voicemail message before calling.

Communicating by email: This option could be the best method if an email is provided and may be more effective in getting a response.

Communicating by fax: Sometimes you only have a fax number. You can write fax inquiries using big type with simple questions.

No contact information: If there is no name or phone, only an address, your only recourse would be to write a letter. If there is no address, only a database, then you can't contact anyone. Just keep submitting and crossing your fingers.

TIMING: HOW LONG DOES IT TAKE TO GET HIRED?

The Office of Personnel Management has recently published a statement requesting that HR offices process applications in 90 days. From the closing date on the announcement until you receive a letter or phone call inviting you to an interview, the time elapsed should be no more than 90 days. Currently, timing for this stage is more like two to four months. We are hopeful that the review and selection process will get faster.

Though there are many different automated application systems, you will see that with one good resume and attention to detail applying on-line, you will be a solid candidate for many job postings.

CHAPTER 6:

INTERVIEW FOR A FEDERAL JOB

Tips for researching, preparation, practice, and, confidence building for successful federal interviews

FEDERAL JOB INTERVIEWS
ARE DIFFERENT EACH TIME

There are many different approaches to interviewing, so this section is intended to help you understand the various methods and to provide some practical tips on preparing!

Managers use many interviewing techniques and processes to develop an understanding of you as a candidate for their position. The interview will depend on the type of position, as well as the information the manager needs to obtain to determine if you are the best "fit" for the position.

Interviews for first-time federal jobseekers are, in general, not any different from those for current federal employees. You may be asked about long-term career goals, your interest in the position and the agency, and your long- and short-term educational plans. Be sure that you are comfortable discussing in a positive manner your current course work, professors, and what you are learning.

Interviews may be conducted in person, over the phone, and may include an interview panel. Interviews may fall into one of several categories, including:

- Behavioral interviewing
- Technical interviewing
- Competency interviewing
- Combination interviewing
- General interviewing

All of the interview methods listed above call for some preparation on your part. However, you need to understand which type of interview you will be participating in. When you are contacted for the interview, it is appropriate for you to request information regarding the type and method of interviewing that will be conducted.

Let's discuss the different interviewing methods listed above:

Behavioral Interviewing:

This employment interview is situational in nature, is intended to discover how interviewees will respond to different situations.

Technical Interviewing:

Technical interviews are focused on providing the selecting official with additional information regarding the technical or functional skills of the applicant.

Competency Interviewing:

In this type of interview, applicants are asked questions to determine their possession of the competencies required for the position. These interviews may be also seem like the behavioral interviews described above.

General Interviewing:

A general interview is based on a variety of questions asked of the applicant, and may cover a variety of issues or concerns. A general interview may also be informal, such as "meeting for coffee" or "let's talk about this."

Combination:

The combination interview may involve any of the three interview techniques above, as well as general interview questions.

INTERVIEW TIPS

BEFORE THE INTERVIEW

- Be prepared!

- Check out the website of the agency you're interviewing with and conduct research (size, services, mission, etc.).

- Prepare a 1-minute response to the "Tell me about yourself" question.

- Know what kind of interview to expect – behavioral, technical, etc. Feel free to ask when scheduling the interview.

- Write five success stories to answer behavioral interview questions ("Tell me about a time when…" or "Give me an example of a time…").

- Prepare answers to the most common interview questions that will present your skills, talents, and accomplishments:
    - Why did you leave or are you leaving your last position?
    - What do you know about our organization?
    - What are your goals?/where do you see yourself in 5 years?
    - What are your strengths and weaknesses?
    - Why would you like to work for this organization?
    - What is your most significant achievement?
    - How would your last boss and colleagues describe you?
    - Why should we hire you?
    - What are your salary expectations?

- And remember that nothing will make you look worse than not knowing what you put on your own resume.

- Have 10 questions prepared for the interviewer, but only ask the ones which were not addressed during your discussion.

- Practice in front of a mirror or with a friend for feedback.

- Have your references' permission. These might be former managers, professors, friends of your family who know you well (but not family members), or people who know you through community service. You want them to be prepared to praise you. It would be beneficial to provide your references with the following information: the job for which you are applying, the name of the organization, and a copy of your resume.

THE INTERVIEW

- Arrive 10 to 15 minutes early for your interview.

- Carry these items to the interview:
  - A copy of your references (for which you already have permission to contact)
  - Paper on which to take notes
  - Directions to the interview site
  - A copy of your DD-214

- Watch your body language and eye contact. Stand and greet your interviewer with a firm handshake. Crossed-arms appear to be defensive, fidgeting may be construed as nervous, and lack of eye contact may be interpreted as an untrustworthy person. Instead, nod while listening to show you are attentive and alert and most importantly, do not slouch.

- Think before you answer, and have a clear understanding of the question. Ask for clarification if needed.

- Express yourself clearly and with confidence, and, without conceit. Keep your answers two to three minutes long.

- Show a sincere interest in the agency and position. You should already know about the organization from your research.

- Focus on what you can contribute to the organization rather than what the employer can do for you. Don't ask about salary or benefits until the employer brings up this topic.

- Do not place blame on or be negative about past employers.

- End the interview on an assumptive note indicating how you feel you are a good fit for the position at hand and how you can make a contribution to the organization. Ask about the next step, as most offers are not extended on the spot.

- Thank the interviewer and ask for a business card to provide you with the necessary contact information.

AFTER THE INTERVIEW

How do you want to be remembered after the interview? You want to stand out in their memory as a great candidate, personable, and with the skills they need. Leave a lasting impression with a friendly handshake and smile.

7 STEPS TO A MEMORABLE INTERVIEW – AND A JOB OFFER

Interview Preparation Tip No. 1 – How do you want to be remembered?
Think about your experiences in terms of what's significant, memorable, or interesting. When the manager or managers get together to review the candidates who were interviewed, they will try to remember each of them in some way. You definitely want to be remembered in some way. It could be an experience, skill, story, style, (not your clothes or body language, hopefully), friendliness, attitude, or confidence. Think about this.

Interview Preparation Tip No. 2 – Write your interview stories.
Write a list of work and non-paid experiences that could be used in a job or informational interview. Be aware that you may not think that certain events are interesting, but others might, so write down all of the possibilities. You can review the list with a friend or partner later to determine which experiences are most interesting. Don't take anything off the list yourself. These "stories" may also be knowledge, skills and abilities statements contained in your federal application. KSA statements are great practice for interview questions and answers.

Example of types of interesting, successful, and memorable experiences:

- Leadership - Team Leader or co-team leader for training, emergency preparation, logistics, or movement

- A success – something you did that saved lives, money, or time; improved morale; increased visibility; or made something happen

- Change – a project you worked on that changed the way things were handled previously. The change resulted in savings of time, effort, money, etc.

- Organizational – leadership or active membership in organizations that bring value to a particular audience

- New initiatives - ideas recommended and implemented

- Problem solving – handled, researched, and resolved a problem for someone or a group – how did you do it and for whom?

Interview Preparation Tip No. 3 – Practice speaking your stories.

After you've written your examples and expanded on them with details, speak your experiences out loud. All speakers and lecturers practice their presentations and briefs before giving them to their audience. Practicing an interview "speech" is just as important. Learn to speak the examples efficiently and with enthusiasm and a smile once in a while if it's appropriate.

- Recite your answers in front of a mirror.

- Rehearse your response with a friend.

- Use a tape recorder and record your answers. Listen to your voice. Are you impressed?

- Videotape yourself with someone asking you the questions. Watch the tape. Look for areas to improve and the positive points of your presentation.

- Consider delivery style, message, body language, and confidence.

Interview Preparation Tip No. 4 – Add the hiring agency's desired skills, knowledge and expertise to your stories.

Review the vacancy announcement or recruitment advertisement for the job you are seeking. Look for the particular skills they require. Here are some examples:

> *Team leader, organization, discipline, working across agencies, dependable, analytical, detail-oriented, problem-solving, advisor, technical assistant, support to professionals.*

The stories you have written should incorporate these skills. The hiring manager is looking for someone who can "do the job." You want to demonstrate through your examples that you can do the job by integrating the skills they desire into your example. You want to PROVE that you can do the job, not just SAY that you can do the job. That's why it's best to give examples of your skills and experiences, rather than just saying, "I'm a good team member, I always meet my deadlines." Anyone can say that. That statement will not be remembered after a 30-minute interview.

Meet TJ Walker, Media and Interview Trainer

These excellent Interview Tips were written by TJ Walker, the producer of *www.mediatrainingworldwide.com* and expert Interview, Speech, Media and Briefing coach from New York City.

Interview Preparation Tip No. 5 – Get ready to answer interview questions.
Be prepared with answers.

At a recent interview training seminar at the National Archives, TJ Walker and I used a video camera and interviewed four Archives Technicians in preparation for promotion to Archives Specialist positions.

Sampling of TJ's interview Questions:

- Tell me about yourself.

- Do you have a memorable example of your work or achievements?

- What's the worst part of the job?

- What are you most proud of in your career?

- What are your greatest strengths?

- If you're at a cocktail party, what would you talk about?

- Do you have any unique talents or specialized knowledge?

- Do you have a sense of your weakness as an employee? What are they? What is the effect of your weakness?

- How are you different from other applicants for this position?

- Why should we hire you?

- Anything else we should know about you?

- What have you been doing in your current job as a specialist?

- Why do you want to be promoted?

- What skills do you have that are not being utilized?

- What do you mean by that?

Interview Tip No. 5 – Research the Agency or Company Before the Interview

Always research information about the agency or company before the interview. Be prepared to ask questions of the interviewer as well as answer questions. You will probably have an opportunity to ask questions.

Here's a list of places you can go to research companies/agencies:

- Website - press releases in particular – this is the latest news of the organization.

- Mission Statement - compare their mission statement to your current organization's mission statement. Be prepared to talk about either yours or their mission statement.

- About Us – read about the organization set-up, key people, size of the organization and when it was established.

- Services / Programs / Mission – what do they do? Who are their major customers? What are their challenges?

Interview Tip No. 6 – Relax, Be Confident, Don't Tense Up Physically

If you are tense, (sitting with your arms tight at your side, shoulders hunched, face downward), the interviewer will not be relaxed either. Practice sitting and talking for the interview.

- Sit on the chair leaning slightly forward – watch the way the interviewer is sitting, but don't look as relaxed as the interviewer. It's better to NOT cross your legs, you can cross your feet instead. Sit up straight and relax your shoulders.

- Use your hands for the interview. Don't sit on your hands!

- Look at the interviewer when speaking and listening to questions. Very important.

- Smile occasionally but not too much.

- Breath regularly - seriously!

- Listen carefully to the questions. This is more difficult than you think.

- Don't tense up your voice to the point that you do not sound like yourself. (At the National Archives interview class the interview subjects talked differently when the camera was on vs. when the camera was off)

- You will become confident with practice, practice, practice.

- Be confident, but not overly confident. Interviewing is never easy.

- Remember that expert speakers practice, prepare speeches, and have coaches. It's okay to walk around the house bragging about yourself.

- You obviously are qualified for the job, or you would not be in the interview. So relax - you can be hired based on your interview!

Interview Tip No. 7 – Know your Message.

- Show the enthusiasm and the skill level that you have.

- Prepare your stories. What happened? Use any knowledge, skills and abilities examples you have written.

- Don't forget the results – talk about the end product!

- Tailor your message for the job.

MORE EXPERT ADVICE

GETTING READY FOR OPEN-ENDED AND BEHAVIORAL QUESTIONS

Quoted From Merit Systems Protection Board Report, The Structured Interview

Managers will ask effective questions. As we've indicated, effective interview questions are based on job analysis to ensure that they are job-related. Effective interview questions are also usually open-ended and behavioral, so that they will elicit useful responses.

Open-ended questions are questions that require the candidate to provide details and cannot be answered in one word (such as "yes" or "excellent"). Such questions are much more effective than closed-ended questions at developing insight into a candidate's experience and abilities. For example, the closed-ended question, "Can you write effectively?" can be answered with an uninformative "Yes" — a response that sheds little light on the candidate's level of performance in this area. An open-ended question such as, "Describe the types of documents you have written, reviewed, or edited," requires the candidate to provide specifics, and provides much more insight into the candidate's writing accomplishments.

There is a place for the closed-ended question. For example, to learn whether a candidate is willing to travel frequently or can start work on a given date, it is perfectly appropriate to ask a closed-ended question.

Behavioral questions are just that: questions that ask the candidate to describe behaviors — responses, actions, and accomplishments in actual situations. The case for the behavioral question is more subtle than the case for open-ended questions. Although research indicates that both behavioral questions ("What did you do?") and hypothetical questions ("What would you do?") can be effective, many researchers and practitioners generally recommend the behavioral question for two reasons.

First, behavioral questions can provide greater insight into how the candidate will perform on the job, because the best predictor of future behavior is past behavior. Second, behavioral questions may be more reliable than hypothetical questions. Because the response can be verified through reference checks or other means, it is more difficult to fabricate an inaccurate or untruthful answer to a behavioral question than to a hypothetical one.

GENERAL SAMPLE INTERVIEW QUESTIONS

All-inclusive
- Tell me about yourself.
- Why should I hire you?
- What about this job interested you?

Putting You on the Spot
- Why are you leaving your current position?

Difficult Questions
- Can you work under pressure?
- Describe a time when your work performance was poor.
- Describe how you've handled a stressful work situation.
- What are your weaknesses?
- Tell me about your worst boss.

Situational Questions
- Describe a situation where your work or an idea was criticized.
- Describe a difficult problem you've had to deal with.
- Tell me about a time when you had to tolerate people with different backgrounds and interests from your own.
- Tell me about a time when you've been particularly effective in relating with others.
- Most of us can look back on a project or idea we were proud of. Can you describe one of yours that you are particularly proud of?
- Describe a time when you used your public speaking skills.

Miscellaneous
- How long would it take for you to make a meaningful contribution to this department?
- Describe yourself as an employee.
- Describe your management style when dealing with staff and co-workers.
- What do you know about our agency?
- How would you describe your standards of performance?
- Do you prefer working with others or alone?
- Define cooperation.

COMPETENCY-BASED SAMPLE INTERVIEW QUESTIONS

Often an interviewer will ask questions that directly relate to a competency required for the position. Here are some examples.

Attention to Detail
Describe a project you were working on that required attention to detail.

Communication
Describe a time when you had to communicate under difficult circumstances.

Conflict Management
Describe a situation where you found yourself working with someone who didn't like you. How did you handle it?

Continuous Learning
Describe a time when you recognized a problem as an opportunity.

Coping
Describe a situation where your results were not up to your supervisor's expectations. What did you do?

Customer Service
Describe a situation in which you demonstrated an effective customer service skill.

Decision Making
Give an example of how you reached a practical business decision by reviewing all the facts.

Decisiveness
Tell me about a time when you had to stand up for a decision you made even though it made you unpopular.

Leadership
Describe a time when you exhibited participatory management.

Negotiating
Tell me about a time during negotiations when your perceptiveness allowed you to make sense of another person's behavior.

WRITE YOUR OWN QUESTIONS FOR THE INTERVIEWERS

Samples:

- What are the biggest challenges for your agency right now?

- Are there any new initiatives or programs that are being set up now?

- What are two of the most important competencies you are seeking in this job?

- What is the geographic area this position will service?

- Is there a large retirement or new recruitment effort going on here?

- How would my performance be evaluated?

- What professional development is available?

- What's next in the hiring and selection process for this job?

FINAL WORDS – TELL THEM YOU WANT THE JOB

If you think the position would be a great match for your experience and interests, do not hesitate to be enthusiastic. You can make a statement like this one: "I really like the sound of this position. I believe I would be able to lead this team and achieve the objectives that you have outlined here today. I hope that I will be selected for this position. I look forward to the next step. And thank you for the opportunity to interview. It was great to meet you and talk with you about your agency."

APPENDIX A

FEDERAL HIRING BENEFITS FOR VETERANS & FAMILY MEMBERS

Advantages in applying for federal jobs for veterans

CAN YOUR MILITARY SERVICE (OR YOUR FAMILY MEMBER'S) GIVE YOU AN ADVANTAGE IN APPLYING FOR FEDERAL JOBS?

Quick answer: Yes, your military service is definitely an advantage. You can apply for jobs that are otherwise open only to current federal employees, and under certain conditions, get preference in hiring including extra points added to your passing score. Under certain conditions family members of veterans and of active duty personnel also receive some advantages in applying for jobs or hiring. Because of these advantages, you can compete against and get selected over first-time private sector applicants!

HIRING PREFERENCE

VETERANS' PREFERENCE

5 points added to your passing score!

Many former service members are eligible for veterans' preference. These applicants are called "preference eligibles." You qualify for 5-point veterans' preference if you meet at least one of these criteria:

1. You served on active duty during a war in a campaign or expedition for which a campaign badge has been authorized.

2. You served on active duty during certain periods defined by specific dates. A list of these dates and more veterans' preference information is available on the CD-ROM.

You must have been discharged under honorable conditions. If an agency is using numerical scores when assessing applicants, these candidates have 5 points added to their passing scores, and must be offered jobs before non-veterans with equal or lesser scores.

10 points added to your application score!

Some military applicants who have been disabled during their service have 10 points added to their passing scores when agencies use numerical scores to assess applicants and must be offered a job before non-veterans with equal or lesser scores. For most jobs, disabled veterans with a compensable service-connected disability of 10 percent or more are listed ahead of all other applicants eligible to be hired. Some family members also may qualify as 10-point preference eligibles. You qualify for 10-point veterans' preference if you meet at least one of these criteria:

- Service members who served on active duty, were separated under honorable conditions, and who establish the present existence of a service-connected disability, or who are receiving compensation, disability retirement benefits, or pension because of a law administered by the Department of Veterans Affairs.

- Unmarried widows or widowers of veterans whose active duty service was during a war, and who served in a campaign or expedition for which a campaign badge was authorized, or during the period beginning April 28, 1952 and ending July 1, 1955.

- Under certain conditions, the spouse of a service-connected disabled veteran or the mother of a service-connected permanently and totally disabled veteran.

Veterans Service Organizations, OPM, and the Department of Labor can provide additional information about these three conditions and more benefits for veterans.

http://www.va.gov/	- Veteran's Service Organizations
http://www.opm.gov/veterans/	- Office of Personnel Management
http://www.dol.gov/vets/welcome.html	- Department of Labor

When agencies use "category ranking" instead of numerical scores to assess applicants, veterans are listed ahead of non-veterans in whatever category their qualifications put them, and must be offered jobs ahead of non-veterans in that category. For most jobs, qualified applicants with a 10 percent or greater service-connected disability are placed at the top of the highest category.

A special advantage granted to 10-point preference eligibles. You can still apply after an announcement has closed!

If you meet the definition of a 10-point preference eligible (see above), you have an advantage not granted to other applicants—you can submit an application for a closed announcement and the agency must accept it. If a selection has not been made when the agency receives your application, it must treat your application as timely. If a selection has been made, the agency must hold your application for consideration for any similar vacancy announced in the calendar quarter following your submission of your application. (Your authority to do this is based on law: 5 USC 3305.)

If you file under this special provision we recommend you email, fax or overnight your application according to the vacancy announcement instructions and include a cover letter stating clearly that you are a 10-point preference veteran applying for this position.

Military Spouse Preference (MSP)

Spouses of active duty members of the armed forces (including the Coast Guard) are eligible for military spouse preference within the Department of Defense when their active duty spouses receive a permanent change in station.

This preference may be used for many vacant positions in DoD, but the jobs must be in the commuting area of the permanent duty station of the sponsor. While all military services operate under the same DoD guidance, there are variations in how they operate their MSP programs. Generally, when the applicant is "Best Qualified" and eligible for MSP, the selecting official must hire the military spouse or have the installation commander approve a decision not to. (NOTE: MSP does not supersede Veterans' Preference.) Always check with the local civilian personnel office in the target area to find out specific policies and application procedures.

APPLICATION PREFERENCE

Veterans' Employment Opportunity Act (VEOA)

The VEOA does not give you an advantage in actual hiring, but it allows you to apply for jobs that are otherwise open only to federal employees! Even if your active duty military service does not qualify you as a "preference eligible," service in the armed forces can work to your advantage. The VEOA allows former service members to apply for vacancies that are open only to current federal civilian employees and those who have "status" because they previously worked as federal civilians. If an agency has announced a vacancy limited to applications from current federal employees and is accepting applications from other Federal agencies, it must accept applications from VEOA applicants.

Being allowed to apply under the VEOA does not give an applicant any advantage in scoring his or her application (does not convey veterans' preference). The advantage you gain is being able to apply for jobs that are not open to the general public. Federal agencies usually have more job listings for internal candidates than for external candidates. To qualify for VEOA you must have served on active duty and have been separated under honorable conditions.

SPECIAL HIRING PROGRAMS

Veterans' Recruitment Appointment (VRA)

The VRA provides a Direct Hire opportunity. This special authority allows agencies to hire you "without competition" for white-collar positions through GS-11 and equivalent jobs under other pay systems. You have to meet basic qualifications, but do not have to be on a list of eligible candidates who are competing for the job. If you submit an application in response to a vacancy announcement you can be hired without having to compete with other applicants.

Get Hired Directly!

The VRA means that you can get hired DIRECTLY by the agency. Your application does not have to be ranked in competition with other applicants--you merely have to be basically qualified for the job. If you know a hiring supervisor, or meet one at a Job Fair, your VRA eligibility could lead to a noncompetitive appointment. Networking can be very helpful for VRA employment opportunities.

The following individuals are eligible for a VRA appointment:

- Disabled veterans

- Veterans who served on active duty in the Armed Forces during a war declared by Congress, in a campaign or expedition for which a campaign badge has been authorized.

- Veterans who, while serving on active duty in the Armed Forces, participated in a military operation for which the Armed Forces Service Medal was awarded.

- Veterans separated from active duty within the past three years.

- There is no minimum service requirement, but the individual must have served on active duty, not active duty for training.

Use of this authority is at the discretion of the agency. Agencies can recruit candidates and make VRA appointments directly, which are initially for two years. Successful completion of the two-year period may lead to a permanent civil service appointment. Persons selected for VRA appointments who have less than 15 years of education must agree to participate in a training or educational program. 15 years means a high school diploma plus three years beyond high school.

30% or more Disabled Veteran Program

Federal agencies have the authority, by law, to give noncompetitive appointments to any veteran who has a service-connected disability of 30 percent or more. Like the VRA, use of this authority is discretionary with the agency. The disability must be officially documented by the Department of Defense or the Department of Veterans Affairs. In addition, the job for which you are hired must be publicly posted.

30% or more Disabled Veterans can also be HIRED DIRECTLY. Networking may pay off here. Having this eligibility can get you the job without competition as long as you are basically qualified.

This authority covers jobs in all grade levels and occupations. You must meet all qualification requirements for any position to which you are appointed. This could include the requirement to achieve a passing score on a written test.

Certain Former Overseas Employees (Family Members)

This hiring authority allows spouses and unmarried children under the age of 23 to be noncompetitively appointed to a stateside position following employment overseas. To qualify, an individual must be a family member of a military sponsor who was officially assigned to an overseas area, have completed 52 weeks of creditable overseas service in an appropriated fund position (for example, not a military base recreation center or bar), have a performance rating of successful or better, and apply within 3 years of returning to the U.S.

Veterans Preference Does NOT Apply to the Following:

- Jobs in the Senior Executive Service (SES)
- Certain medical occupations in the Department of Veterans Affairs (VA is under a separate personnel system—Title 38)
- Retired members of the armed forces UNLESS
  - They are disabled veterans or
  - They retired below the rank of major or equivalent
- Scientific or professional jobs at or above GS-9 do not have "float to the top" provisions for disabled veterans with 10% or greater disability

---

INDEX

MILITARY TO FEDERAL CAREER GUIDE, 2ND EDITION

FEDERAL RESUME WRITING FOR VETERANS

A

B

C

recommended search techniques to find vacancy announcements, 86–87

Usernames, 49

V

W

ABOUT THE AUTHOR

— Kathryn Troutman

KATHRYN TROUTMAN
President and Founder, The Resume Place, Inc.™, 1973 to present
Federal Career Coach™
Certified Federal Job Search Trainer
Certified Federal Resume Writer & Coach
Certified Career Management Coach (CCMC)

Kathryn Troutman wrote the first book on federal resume writing in 1996 – the *Federal Resume Guidebook*. This book and resume style became the industry standard for federal HR and everyone who wants to apply for a federal job. Ms. Troutman has since written *Ten Steps to a Federal Job* and, with her daughter Emily, *The Student's Federal Career Guide*. Both books won Best Career Book of the Year by Publisher's Marketing Association.

Ms. Troutman designed the first-ever Certified Federal Job Search Training (CFJST) program based on the Ten Step curriculum. Now, career counselors are teaching the federal job search program in more than 100 military TAP and Spouse Employment Career Transition classes today! The President and Founder of www.resume-place.com, she and her professional writers provide expert writing and consulting services to more than 1,000 clients per year. Ms. Troutman is also a leading federal career trainer in more than 50 government agencies each year, and she is the Government/Public Service Board federal career coach for www.monster.com. Kathryn lives in Baltimore, MD and is the proud mother of three children who are successful in their careers!

FOR MORE INFORMATION ABOUT VETERANS FEDERAL RESUME WRITING AND CONSULTING SERVCES

The Resume Place, Inc.
89 Mellor Avenue, Baltimore, MD 21228
(410) 744-4324 or (888) 480-8265 | Fax: (410) 744-0112
www.resume-place.com

VETERANS FEDERAL CAREER TRAINING
www.resume-place.com/training/

FREE FEDERAL CAREER RESOURCES AND TOOLS
www.resume-place.com/resources/

CHAPTER 1

THE RESUME PLACE, INC.

FEDERAL CAREER RESOURCES FOR FEDERAL JOBSEEKERS BY KATHRYN TROUTMAN

Military to Federal Career Guide & CD-ROM, 2nd Ed.   **$18.95 + $8.00 postage**
ISBN 978-0-9824190-2-1, 8 ½ x 11, 130 pages, soft cover,
Bulk purchases available for Veteran's Organizations
Military to Federal Resume Writing Guide. This book is for veterans who need to learn how to write a federal resume translating military skills and experiences into keywords for federal jobs. Samples in the Outline Format with keywords and accomplishments. Easy to read federal resumes. Plus CD-ROM with more than 25 samples in the Outline Format.

Federal Resume Guidebook & CD-ROM, 4th Ed.   **$38.95 + $8.00 postage**
ISBN 1-56370-925-2, 8 ½ x 11, 400 pages, soft cover
The leading federal resume writing guide for current federal employees or government contractors. More than 20 more sample federal resumes in Word to use as templates! Specialized chapters on Senior Executive Service applications, converting a scientific CV to a federal resume and insight for writing an IT Specialist, HR Specialist, Program & Management Analyst, Wage Grade (Trades), Contract Specialist, and Administrative federal resume.
*The CD-ROM for this book is available only through The Resume Place, www.resume-place.com.

Ten Steps to a Federal Job & CD-ROM, 2nd Ed.   **$28.95 + $8.00 postage**
ISBN 0-9647025-3-3, 8 x 10, 240 pages, soft cover
Won Careers Best Book of the Year, 2003, Publisher's Marketing Association
Great book for the first-time federal applicant, a private industry application or government contractor who is writing their first federal resume.
20 more sample federal resumes for private industry to federal jobseekers, plus KSAs.

Ten Steps to a Federal Job – Jobseeker Guide, 4th Ed.   **$18.95 + $7.00 postage**
ISBN 0-9824190-3-1, 120 pages, 8 ½ x 11, soft cover
Releasing June 2010
Bulk purchases available for Ten Step Training programs.
Popular handout in Military Career Transition Centers with Air Force, Navy, Army, US Coast Guard and National Guard transition centers throughout the world.

Student's Federal Career Guide & CD-ROM   **$8.00 + $7.00 postage**

Written with Emily K. Troutman
ISBN 0-9647025-6-8, 185 pages, 5 x 7, soft cover
Won Careers Best Book of the Year, 2004, Publisher's Marketing Association
Just returned to college or finished a certification program to advance or change your career?
This book is a MUST. Emphasizes courses, training, projects, internships, team projects. Your federal resume should feature your education. Samples in this book will help you change careers using your new degree!

Creating Your High School Resume, 3nd Ed.   **$16.95 + $7.00 postage**

ISBN 1-56370-902-3, 180 pages, 8 ½ x 11, soft cover
For high school students who need a resume for jobs and college applications! Outstanding samples, case studies, and job search stories for high school juniors and seniors. Teacher's guide, PowerPoints available for instructors.

ORDER BOOKS ONLINE @
WWW.RESUME-PLACE.COM

A RECOMMENDED WEBSITE FOR
VETERAN'S FEDERAL EMPLOYMENT INFORMATION

www.fedshirevets.gov/job/veterans.aspx